THE POWER OF A GRACEFUL LEADER

The POWER of a

GRACEFUL LEADER

FLOW
INTEGRATION
ALIGNMENT

ALEXSYS THOMPSON

LIONCREST
PUBLISHING

THE POWER OF A GRACEFUL LEADER

ISBN 978-1-5445-0498-8 *Paperback*
    978-1-5445-0499-5 *Ebook*

To the grace within all of us

CONTENTS

Dear Reader...9

Introduction 13

1. What Grace Is.. 33

2. The Tenets of Graceful Leadership 57

3. Why Gratitude Is the Entry Point to Grace................. 103

4. Uniting Self and Soul.. 127

5. Use Grace to Distinguish Story from Fact.................... 149

6. Grace in the Face of Conflict 169

7. How Grace Can Transform a Company's Culture 181

8. Create Your Unique Path to Graceful Leadership 201

9. How to Talk about Grace in Your Workplace 229

Pulling It All Together 243

Gratitudes 249

About Alexsys.. 255

DEAR READER

Welcome—I am honored and so glad you are here. The process of birthing this book took place over a couple of decades, the actual organizing and writing of it has happened over the last year, and as I am completing the final edits to this book, we are eight weeks into the COVID-19 pandemic.

This is an unprecedented time for leaders on all levels. Daily, I am having conversations with executive teams where head count, pay, benefits, how we work, and revenue are all suspended in air, with hopes that not one falls from the sky. The amount of details and strategy being asked of leaders is intense, to say the least, and graceful leadership has never been more paramount than right now in our modern world. It means more to me now than ever to share with you the stories, ideas, and practices within these pages, as grace is the path forward to a more compassionate and love-centered world.

We all have a "why" that unlocks the being we are here to live into. I have made the unlocking of my why a life practice. It is often said that we teach and share the lessons we have lived through. Finally, in my early fifties, I feel ready and wanting to share my why and the many journeys it took to get here. This is not to say I am at an end of anything; rather, I'm at the beginning of so many things. This is a moment of reflection and focus to document and share the lessons I have learned and refined daily to live a graceful and grace-filled life.

The stories I share along the way are not of any one person, but rather a compilation of approaches and people I have had the honor to work with. I have created various avatars to represent the patterns I have seen reoccurring in so many leaders and to help demonstrate concepts or ideas. Stories help us to make things relatable, and this body of work is all about application and integration. Through these stories, my hope for you as you move through this book is that you are able to grasp the tenets that support you in really diving deep into your grace center. I hope that you will find the topics deeply relatable and that they create a stir within you—a whisper from your deepest being to awaken into your grace center and learn to deploy grace in all areas of your life.

Some have asked why I choose to focus this book on leaders, and the question makes me smile. This answer came to me several decades ago when I was sitting in a presentation about talent and leadership. It was one statistic from Gallup that changed everything for me: the simple fact that, on average, a leader directly impacts at least twelve other humans through leadership—often many more. I sat there realizing the power that someone in leadership has just by doing the trickle-down math. I decided to focus my education on leadership and completed my bachelor's and master's later in life in just that: leadership. I have come to believe that we all need and should be able to count on great leadership. That belief is not realized as much as I would like to see in our current work. COVID-19 seems to be putting a spotlight on our gaps in this area in all facets of our American society.

So, let's do the math. If just 100 people read this book and step into their grace as a result, they will have a positive impact on at least 1,200 people. Then, if just half of those 1,200 people embrace the graceful tenets as well, the impact rises to 7,200. If half of those people then pass on the lessons, the impact expands to 43,200. And on and on and on. With these ever-expanding ripples of graceful leaders, in short order we would all have models of what grace is in leadership, many of the either-or beliefs we have would fall away, and we would all be much more free to live in our grace centers and still hold our personal power. That is the kind of world I aspire to live in, and I hope you will join me in this movement of graceful leadership.

Thank you for the commitment you made to purchase and open this book and read this far along with me. I know the value of our time, and I do not take it lightly that you are investing in yourself here with me. I look forward to our time among these pages. Entering into your grace center isn't always easy, but it is always worth it.

INTRODUCTION

WHO BENEFITS FROM GRACEFUL LEADERSHIP? EVERYONE.

Do you have an established career as an effective leader yet feel as if something is missing?

Do you feel as if you've sold your soul in the name of professional success?

Have you been taught to forge ahead at all costs, never showing weakness, abiding by the mantra "Results, results, results!"?

Are you partitioning off parts of yourself at work? Do you have a strict divide between your personal life and your professional life?

Do you have a gnawing feeling that you're not connecting as deeply as you could with your peers and subordinates? Do you not feel seen or heard? Have you ever thought, *If they only knew me!*

Do you ever look in the mirror and wonder how you got here? Do you worry that your path has led you to something you don't even want?

If you answered yes to any of these questions, you're not alone. I've seen these patterns over and over again throughout my practice, within all levels of leadership. The good news is that there *is* a better way, and together we can find it. It's called graceful leadership.

HOW GRACE CAN HELP

When people hear the word *grace*, they often think of religion. While religion can play a role in grace for some leaders, grace, as defined here, is not about religion. Rather, grace is *the* practical *expression of a loving, connected compassion with self and others*. It is the ability to see yourself in the other.

Grace is beauty and strength combined. It has a warrior energy to it. Grace does not equal doormat. Rather, a graceful leader has a power that is accountable. Graceful leadership offers a two-way street of connection: the graceful leader is felt and seen by the people, community, and organization they are leading, and those who experience the graceful leader are similarly left feeling seen and heard.

Graceful leadership is the most integrated form of leadership. It allows you to form a bridge between personal and professional, align yourself to your purpose, and adapt as required for each unique situation.

The journey into our gracefulness is a gritty one—bumpy, messy, and one of the most refining experiences we will travel into. The humanness that is us creates a journey that will be revisited and refined over one's lifetime. Entering into your inner grace is one of the most accountable journeys you will ever take.

INTEGRATION: BRIDGING THE INTERNAL DIVIDE

The tipping point of becoming a graceful leader is first expressing loving, connected compassion for yourself. When you offer this compassion to yourself, you give yourself the opportunity to become more integrated. Instead of having several different versions of yourself—the you at work, the you at home, the you in your community, and so on—there is only the one unified, connected you.

I've worked with countless people who were toxic, nasty people at work. Then I would witness them in a different area of their life—volunteering at the local food bank, biking at the fitness club, or simply shopping at the grocery store—and I would discover that they had the most compassionate hearts. *What the heck is happening here?* I asked myself each time I came across this pattern. *Why can't these leaders be compassionate in their professional lives as well as their personal lives?*

This imbalance works in the opposite direction as well, with people needing to bring aspects of their professional selves into their personal lives. I've seen many people, especially women, who are powerful leaders at work. Then, at home, they become doormats, abdicating all power and responsibility to their spouse. In the past, I certainly needed better boundaries in my personal life. I let my former spouse speak to me in ways that I never would've tolerated at work. If a peer or even a boss had said some of those things to me, I would've chewed them up and spit them out for lunch. This incongruence made me unpredictable, resulting in confusion for me and those around me.

We're taught that we can be only one thing at a time: compassionate or powerful. It's a lie. You don't have to be one or the other. You can be *all of you*. In fact, you will be infinitely more powerful if you embrace the wholeness of yourself.

A lack of balance between one's personal and professional lives is a huge internal stressor. Segregating yourself into different "yous" is exhausting and can lead to emotional breakdowns and serious physical ailments. It's one of the main reasons people come to me, looking for another way. They can feel their personal and professional selves grating against each other, and they want to figure out how to bridge the two, forming a holistic, consistent version of themselves. Grace is what builds the bridge.

ALIGNMENT: THE ONE YOU

Grace with yourself is a meeting of your internal and external landscapes. It is a congruency between what you do and who you are. When you become a graceful leader, you understand your desires and your purpose for being on the planet, and you act in accordance. Aligning yourself to your underlying purpose in this way allows you to achieve synergy of self, and it holds you accountable.

For me, my driving purpose is to create safe places for souls to show up. When we have an environment of safety, we all get to show up with our full brilliance, allowing us to achieve the greatest results. That purpose is who I am—my internal landscape. It is the filter I lead through. I am only human, and so my external world—what I do—does not always match that internal landscape. To create the congruency, I am always asking myself, "Am I creating safety? If not, what do I need to do to change that?" By returning to this compass, I can ensure that who I am and what I do are aligned more often than not.

One cannot be graceful without being aligned. This will require an honest inventory of where you are and where you wish to be. The judgment you place around the divide will be explored and over time redefined to create the balance and love that are required internally to uncover your purpose, the one you feel and crave access to. It is only when we dedicate ourselves to our purpose that we can fully unlock the power of the graceful leader.

FLOW: ADAPTING FLUIDLY

Grace allows you to adapt to any given situation in a fluid, intuitive manner. Graceful leaders are never stuck in one position. They are wholly integrated—mind, body, and soul. They have access to all that they are, at all times. This means that they can call forth whatever aspects of themselves are needed for a particular situation. In one moment, they can draw on their compassion to comfort a team member who has suffered a personal loss, and in the next, they can lean into their firm confidence to deliver an important presentation. Because of this flow between roles and strengths, graceful leaders have far more tools to employ in every situation.

You may have heard the term *servant leadership* before. This view of leadership upholds that a leader's primary role is to serve. Very rarely does the leader need to lead from the front. Instead, they spend their time in the back, removing barriers, creating opportunities, and generally supporting their team. Graceful leadership builds upon and extends this idea of servant leadership. The graceful leader understands that nine times out of ten, they will be in the back serving. In that rare instance that they need to lead from the front or side, they will flow seamlessly into that position and adapt their leadership style to fit the needs of the situation. The epitome of a graceful leader is knowing where to be, when to be there, and how to be there. It's like having a playbook in football, where you know exactly where you're supposed to be on the field.

The infinity symbol is a good representation of this concept of flow.

The graceful leader is constantly flowing from one part of the symbol to another. At any given moment, the leader understands where they are needed along the infinity symbol. Instead of trying to push or pull people along, the graceful leader's power lies in being in the right position at the right time for the situation. The followers will naturally cluster around wherever the leader is, like a flock of birds flying in a V.

The graceful leader is present in the moment and understands when to take action and when to be still. Many leaders attain results by force, by pushing and driving. Yet, though it is a skill not many acquire or master, stillness can be a leader's greatest asset. In a crisis, you might need to take charge and employ traditional command-and-control leadership methods. If a normally high-performing team member begins struggling, you might instead need to be still, sitting with that person and giving them the needed space to open up about the issue. Grace encourages this flow between action and stillness.

GRACEFUL LEADERS AMONG US

The easiest way to understand graceful leadership is to look at examples of it. Graceful leadership can take many different forms. Despite their seeming differences, Rose Marcario, Martin Luther King Jr., Hamdi Ulukaya, Jane Goodall, and Maya Angelou are all excellent examples of graceful leaders.

> *My whole self is here. My values, my*
> *passion, my sense of urgency.*
> —ROSE MARCARIO

As Patagonia CEO Rose Marcario herself attests, she brings her whole self to the table. She is an integrated individual who has aligned herself with her purpose of protecting the environment. As Marcario has said, "Caring for our planet is not in conflict with running a successful business." In 2016, while under Marcario's leadership, Patagonia donated 100 percent of its Black Friday sales to grassroots environmental organizations. In addition to charitable giving, Patagonia has worked toward sustainability, both in terms of production and through programs like Worn Wear, which encourages reusing preowned clothing to reduce overall consumption. In pursuit of this purpose, Marcario has demonstrated flow, adapting to the current cultural climate. With this fluidity, she has led Patagonia to make bold, nontraditional moves for a company, like endorsing political candidates. And alongside all her work for the planet, she has indeed run a successful business, with profits having quadrupled during her tenure.

You want to be integrated with yourself, and the way to be integrated with yourself is be sure that you meet every situation of life with an abounding love.
—MARTIN LUTHER KING JR., "LOVING YOUR ENEMIES" SPEECH

Martin Luther King Jr. expressed superhuman levels of grace. He integrated his identities as minister and activist, simultaneously demanding change and accountability while still holding love for his enemies. He aligned himself to his purpose of furthering civil rights and spoke often of how one must dedicate oneself to a purpose greater than self. He supported his peers and followers and just as easily flowed forward, leading from the front at a time when it was dangerous to do so.

People gravitated to MLK for a variety of reasons. Some of these people could have easily been on opposite sides of the conversation, yet MLK was able to unite them. He had remarkable skill in balancing polarizing dualities—both in himself and in others. In the face of violence and hate, he urged his followers to nonviolence, peace, and love. He showed that it was possible to be angry and peaceful, to want change and not be bitter, to stand against your enemies and hold love for them in your heart. This ability to rise above duality is a clear sign of grace.

> *Business is not always seen as a force for*
> *good, but it can and must become one.*
> —HAMDI ULUKAYA

One of the things that sets Hamdi Ulukaya, CEO of Chobani, apart from other business leaders is his commitment to people. He grew up in a village in rural Turkey, and though his current life is arguably quite different from his roots, he has retained and integrated the lessons from his early life into his career. His early experiences seeing working-class families struggle while the wealthy got richer instilled in him an ideal that profits and paying people good wages need not be mutually exclusive. His purpose is improving his employees' lives and their communities, and he has aligned himself to that purpose by compensating employees fairly as well as starting a profit-sharing program so that the employees share in the business's success. He has said, "When you share success, it grows."

The most important thing is to actually think about what you do. To become aware and actually think about the effect of what you do on the environment and on society. That's key, and that underlies everything else.

—Jane Goodall

Few have lived their lives aligned with their purpose to the extent of Jane Goodall. From an early age, she had a remarkable clarity of purpose. She focused on a particular species in a specific part of our world—chimpanzees in Africa—and she dedicated her whole life practice to her study, even going so far as to live among the chimps. She quite literally molded her external landscape so that it perfectly matched her internal purpose. She was thoughtful and intentional, thinking about how her actions aligned—or did not align—with her identified purpose.

Where other researchers put clinical distance between themselves and their subjects, Goodall allowed all of herself to show up—her emotional side as well as her scientific side. For instance, instead of assigning chimpanzees numbers, she named them. As a result of her integration, she was able to recognize and document social behaviors, personalities, and feelings among the chimps that previous research had neglected. She also developed a fierce commitment to these creatures. Grace and ferocity may appear to be incompatible, yet grace can be powerful and ferocious beyond belief.

Later in life, Goodall allowed herself to flow to new positions in order to best further her purpose. She founded the Jane Goodall Institute, a global wildlife and environment conservation organization. She wrote books. She began public speaking. She adapted so that she could better raise humanity's awareness of the creatures with whom we share the planet. Throughout all her shifts, she remained graceful.

> *A Woman in harmony with her spirit is like a river flowing. She goes where she will without pretense and arrives at her destination prepared to be herself and only herself.*
> —MAYA ANGELOU

Maya Angelou was a master of flow. She understood that words hold power and that silence does as well. Her use of stillness was apparent in her readings, where her pauses and silences spoke as much as her words. She allowed listeners the time to interpret and inhabit her poetry. She flowed seamlessly from speech to silence, to powerful effect.

Angelou embodied the concepts of integration and alignment as well. She certainly achieved a deep connection between her internal and external landscapes. As a poet, she put her inner being into words that she shared with the world, aligning herself to her purpose. She gave herself compassion such that she could be who she was, with no mask—one integrated, whole version of herself—and she extended that compassion to others as well.

Martin Luther King Jr., Jane Goodall, and Maya Angelou are proof that graceful leadership provides both personal and professional benefits. If nothing else, there is no denying that these three individuals were hugely influential, with their impact still resonating today. If you take the lessons of this book to heart, you too have the opportunity to awaken the grace that is and has always been with you.

WHY GRACE?

Grace is the key to sustained happiness, more fulfilling work, and performance that impacts the world.

The world is becoming faster. We are simultaneously more and less connected than ever before. We can more easily maintain relationships across thousands of miles, yet too often, our new connectedness is an illusion hiding an ever-widening divide. We bury our heads in our phones and are not present with one another in person. We are constantly on the go, looking for our next dopamine hit.

Because of these technological changes, time spent in conscious focus is more important than ever. We must take the time to slow down and access our self-awareness, and we must be intentional about how we build and grow our relationships. Grace can help with that.

In the scope of leadership, we currently have the most generations in the workforce that we've ever had. Baby boomers are working alongside Gen Xers and millennials, and Generation Z is on its way in. Although it's easy to segment and complain about different generations, it's far more productive to adapt and improve communication to bridge generational gaps. The workforce is changing, and leaders must learn to lead inside more dynamic work environments. Graceful leadership works across generations, across geographic lines, across gender, across whatever divides you can imagine. Graceful leadership is human leadership.

The journey into grace isn't always easy. It requires vulnerability and work. It's worth it, though. I know because I've been where you are now. I operated from a results-at-all-costs mentality, wringing every last drop out of my team. I was successful, and I was miserable. It's taken me years, but through the tenets I outline in this book, I have been able to step into my grace and reach the place of being able to write this book. I think we often come into the universe with a pain or a healing that we're supposed to process so that we can then teach others. For me, that's graceful leadership.

Throughout the book I'll be sharing personal stories about my own journey into grace as well as themes I've witnessed among my clients, shared in story format. For now, I'll give you the CliffsNotes version of my story to show you where I've been and how grace has transformed my life.

MY JOURNEY WITH GRACE

For the astrologers out there, I'm a Taurus. I'm also a firstborn. For me, the stereotypes hold true. Stubborn, bull-headed, assertive—that's me.

From an early age, I worked in a man's world—first in a sheet metal shop and then as a car salesperson. I quickly became a high performer. At the car dealership, I was the number-one salesperson multiple times. I succeeded because I mirrored the men around me. I used their behavior as a calibration tool for what was expected of me in a business environment. I didn't realize that I was hardwiring harmful lessons into my psyche.

The first such lesson was that there was no time for feelings. I learned to see feelings as a sign of weakness and a waste of time—something that didn't belong in the workplace. The second lesson was that coworkers shouldn't build relationships. When I tried to form deeper friendships with several of my male coworkers, my efforts always met a brick wall. The guys were happy to grab some beer and tacos with me;

that was as deep as our friendships got. We were friendly, not friends.

I was taught to not feel, or at least to not express my feelings, and I was taught to suppress the part of me that craved nurturing, deep relationships. Essentially, during these formative experiences, I was taught to stifle my feminine energy. My femininity was reduced to a tool that I deployed externally. Truly, it was no longer femininity. It was sexuality. Sex sells, and I worked in a culture of "Results, results, results!" so I used what I had. Although I wanted to be seen for my technical knowledge—I *loved* talking cars— most couldn't see past my exterior. As a result, I learned early that a cute outfit and a sassy attitude would close a sale far faster than any technical knowledge I had worked to acquire.

Later in life, I became a single mom, and all the harmful lessons I learned early in my work career seeped into my personal life. My kids needed me to be a results-driven *and* vulnerable mother, and I only really achieved half of that. I succeeded in teaching them to be who they are unapologetically, to be the victors of their lives, and to be accountable. These were fantastic key competencies for them to learn. Just as important—and notably absent—was education in how to form healthy relationships. While I had been married twice, neither relationship had been a healthy model for my children. Additionally, I was so used to smothering my emotions at work that I did it at home as well, and I was not as emotionally available to my children as I wish I had been.

My kids and I grew up together in many ways, because in my late twenties and early thirties, I started developing my self-awareness and asking the all-important question, "Who am I, really?" As I explored further, I gravitated to practices of gratitude. I had a lot of starts and stops. It took me a good six years to get to a place where I had a faithful, robust practice of gratitude.

Gratitude became my door to grace. As I found more and more to appreciate, I softened. I grew less intense at work and connected more to the human, relational elements of leadership. I began to nurture my feminine energy (distinct from feminine sexuality) that had been stifled for so long. The harsh judgments I had for myself started to melt away, and in turn, so did my judgments of others. The results were obvious. I felt more satisfied and fulfilled, and so did my work colleagues.

After a decade of work on myself, I left my corporate job at the time and started working in the human capital space, eventually moving into executive coaching. Over the next fifteen years, I saw the same pattern I'd lived emerge again and again in my clients. Client after client was struggling with the same critical missing piece: grace. And so now here I am, writing this book about grace.

THE PROMISE OF THIS BOOK

As you move among these pages, it is my intention that you see the graceful leader within you and begin or continue (depending on where you are now) your leadership development. The journey we will take together in this book is to explore how you can manifest the power of your grace with your gifts as you lead yourself and others into our new world.

Through the tenets outlined in this book, you'll have an opportunity to understand how to be graceful to self. You will learn to live your life with more alignment, integration, and flow. You will find new tools for leading and will get firsthand examples of how to apply those tools at work. If you wish to explore any concepts further, I include relevant resources at the end of each chapter. Some resources apply to multiple chapters and will be included more than once. With these resources, you will have a broad foundation to draw on when the terrain gets rocky, and with grace, you will learn to appreciate those rocky periods as a gift—a chance to polish off what you think you know about who you are or are not.

As a by-product of your individual journey with grace, you will help to create a new culture in your environment—in your company, your home, and your community. Leading with grace means learning how to be engaged and accountable. When you demonstrate these traits, those around you will mirror them back to you. With more engagement and accountability come great results and more innovation.

This book will be a lifelong guide for you. Sometimes after we read a book or go through a class, we mentally check it off our list and think, *Good job! All done!* Then we never return to the material. That isn't this book. This book is designed for you to return to it.

On your first read, you'll likely be drawn to some tenets and sections more than others. That's okay. Feel free to focus your attention on what you're drawn to the most. Better for you to fully integrate just one tenet into your life than gain superficial—and easily forgettable—understanding of all six tenets. Then, a year from now, five years from now, ten years from now, you can pick the book up again. You will be a different you, so you will interface with the material differently and gain new insights.

Whether it is your first read or your tenth, I am so incredibly humbled you have invested your time here with me on the best investment you will ever make—*you!*

CHAPTER 1

WHAT GRACE IS

Author and thought leader Richard Rudd has described *grace* as "careful without being fearful, caring without being over-bearing, candid without being cruel." Grace emerges through your suffering as you become aware and accountable for your responses. Graciousness is an experience we have when we awaken to our emotional life and are accountable for how we share that emotional life in our relationships. Perhaps more so in leadership than in many of the relationships we have the privilege of being part of, grace is crucial. As we lead a diverse collection of people toward a common goal, we will be called upon to do so in many different ways. Some ways will be natural to us, and others a stretch; grace is the bridge.

Grace is the experience of a loving, connected compassion within yourself, and graceful leadership is grace in action. Grace is manifested differently for everyone. You can recognize it when you feel it. For me, it's as if my soul looks in the mirror, and my eyes look back, and I say, "Oh, there you are." It's a gentle whisper and a deep recognition. Grace makes me feel whole, completely seen. Grace is transcendent. Even the simple act of witnessing grace secondhand is a powerful experience.

WITNESSING GRACE FOR THE FIRST TIME: GRACE ELIMINATES DUALITY

In my late twenties, I moved from Vermont to Texas to work at a missing kids' organization, and I met Ashley's parents, Erin and Samuel. You might think, *I can only imagine what it would be like to have a missing child*. Truly, we can't even imagine it. It is a living hell. Erin and Samuel were two such parents to go through that hell, and then they entered a new level of hell when their daughter was found murdered. Yet even in the midst of their pain, Erin and Samuel were the epitome of grace. I consider myself fortunate to have been witness to the grace they extended to each other and those around them.

There is one moment that stands out in my mind. I was sitting in the kitchen, and Erin and Samuel were in the living room, participating in marriage counseling as part of the grieving process.

"I feel really bad for Scott," Erin said.

Time stopped for me in that moment. I instinctively knew that I was observing something that I might never see again. Because Scott was the man accused of murdering Ashley.

"He must have been in a really bad place to feel that murdering our daughter was a good idea," Erin continued.

I could see them from my spot in the kitchen, and it was clear that Samuel felt confused and conflicted by his wife's statement. *How can you dare say that when our daughter is dead?* he seemed to be thinking.

"He's going to be held accountable," Samuel said sternly.

"Yes," Erin agreed. "He must be held accountable, and I also forgive him."

It was a life-changing moment for me to witness this woman in deep stress and unimaginable pain extend love and forgiveness to the man who most of us would say had inflicted that pain. I wish that everybody could sit in that moment like I did and feel the raw, amazing, beautiful power of this grace. All duality evaporated. That blending of grace and accountability showed me that you can forgive someone while simultaneously holding them accountable for the consequences of their behavior. It doesn't have to be one or the other. You can hold anger and grief and love and compassion all at once.

In my work with missing children, I'd witnessed many other couples who fell into patterns of condemnation instead of grace. Most damaging of all, they would blame each other for the death of their child, at times leading to divorce or marriages in name only. Erin and Samuel, in contrast, are still married today, and in my opinion, the grace they showed each other played a critical role in their staying together. Grace strengthens relationships, while blame tears them down.

Erin and Samuel weren't enlightened masters or spiritual gurus. They were just regular people, like you and me. Grace isn't picky. It's available to anyone who seeks to embrace it. It is within each of us. I hadn't yet embraced grace in my own life; however, because of Erin and Samuel, my eyes had been opened, and I began witnessing grace in other areas of my life.

HARD-TO-SWALLOW FEEDBACK: GRACE IN THE UNEXPECTED

Starting from when I was very young, people would tell me that I was too much—too smart, too loud, too assertive, too bossy, too this, too that, too *everything*. So I dialed it all back. Then, I got into leadership roles, and all those traits were turned back on to achieve results. Because I'd been trying to hide them for so long, I didn't have any discipline in how they showed up. As a result, I had all the raw talent for leading and no guardrails to help me navigate how to lead effectively in all areas.

At work, sometimes people would call me a "trailblazer." When they used that word with men, it was a compliment; with me, it came across differently. It was essentially a nice way for them to say "bitch," and plenty of people used that word to describe me as well. When I look back, there were certainly times when I *acted* like a jerk. It's not who I truly was, though. I looked tough from the outside; inside, though, I felt like a marshmallow.

For a long time, I was blind to my behavior, as if I were sleepwalking. Later, I recognized what I was doing and felt ashamed and guilty. I didn't see any other options, though. I didn't have any role models to use for guidance. People always told me what I *shouldn't* be; they never showed me what I *should* be. Others had given me this name tag of "bitch," and so I assumed that identity. People put labels on us all the time, and especially when we're young, we assume those labels for ourselves. If someone says you're pretty, then you assume you're pretty. If someone says you're ugly, you assume you're ugly. We internalize these external judgments and accept them as the truth, until something happens that encourages us to investigate and question them.

For me, "bitch" became like a protective armor. I took on a mindset of "Well, if that's what I am and I'm getting the results I'm supposed to, then that's just what I have to do." Besides, I saw men act the same way all the time. Why should I have to play by different rules? Oddly, not much has changed—I assist female executives in navigating this topic weekly.

Many years after my experience with Erin and Samuel, one of my team members started to fall behind. In characteristically direct fashion, I told her, "Here are your numbers. Here's where they need to be. Whatever you're doing, it's not working. You have thirty days to fix it." Done. Problem solved.

As I headed to the elevators to get to a meeting, my boss pulled me aside. He'd overheard the conversation. "What you just did, that's not okay," he said. "Yes, we need results, but it's not going to be at the expense of being ugly to people. If all you want is results, then you need to find another job."

He also told me, "You need to understand where people are." It turned out that the teammate in question was going through a horrific situation at home. Though she'd talked to the company's owners about it, she hadn't talked to me. And why would she? I had not created a safe space where she felt comfortable opening up to me in that way. As a result, I didn't have needed context. I didn't understand where she was; I only cared about where *I* wanted her to be.

I wouldn't call that boss a graceful leader, yet in that moment of feedback, he extended grace to me. He was firm without being aggressive, direct while being respectful and kind. He certainly didn't set a ticking mental time bomb by threatening to fire me in x number of days if I didn't get my act together. He simply saw the situation more clearly than I did, and he was asking me to do better.

I had a hard time reconciling his words, though, because my results *were* outstanding. Throughout the span of my career, I had even won awards for my results—the National Center for Missing Children Award in 1998, the Texans for Equal Justice Award in 1999, and multiple sales awards for exceeding my goals. How could you argue with that? For years, it had been ingrained in me that results were all that mattered. No one had ever spoken to me about all the other aspects of leadership, like empathy, compassion, and simple relationship building beyond the "job." (All I saw was that it was just about numbers, and I had that figured out.)

If it weren't for my experience with Ashley's parents, I don't think I would have been able to accept my boss's feedback. I probably would have gotten belligerent and fought back. However, if Ashley's parents could forgive the man who had murdered their daughter while still holding him accountable for his actions, then what business did I have clinging to this supposed duality that I could either get results or be kind? For perhaps the first time, I considered that I could do both. I could tell someone that their behavior needed to change while simultaneously extending them caring compassion. My boss had shown me an example of how to do just that.

That moment became an anchoring point. Somehow, it all just clicked. I understood that there was a better way. Even still, I felt confused, embarrassed, and a little angry and defensive. Though I had gotten a glimpse of the path forward, I had no idea yet where it would lead or what to do next. I thought, *Okay, now what?* This curiosity—the simple act of questioning what I previously took for granted—was an integral step in my path into gracefulness.

Becoming a graceful leader isn't like flipping a light switch. It takes time. Grace is about meeting people where they are, including yourself. I'm not proud of all my past behavior. I'm done feeling guilty and ashamed for it, though. Grace isn't guilt or shame. It's acceptance and love. Acting like a jerk was where I *used* to be. Because I was willing to acknowledge my failings and work to move forward, I would move into becoming a graceful leader. A large part of my start on this journey was to take a relationship inventory—a real one. I had to be brave and look at past and current relationships and own my part of what worked and did not—no more blame and no more shame. This activity took about a year of conversations, cleanup, and amends where needed. This clean slate was the foundation I needed for the rest of my journey. Grace is clean, clear, and owes no debts.

THE DANCE OF A GRACEFUL LEADER

Graceful leadership is like a ballet. Ballet dancers are the epitome of grace to me because they are fluid yet intentional with their movement. When I watch a ballet, a sense of peace comes into my being, one moment building on another as the dancers take you on a journey that flows with great power. Graceful leadership is similar, with the leader flowing to wherever they need to be, when they need to be there.

Graceful leadership is intentional and powerful, not willy-nilly or weak. At first it must be done consciously, until you've practiced it so much that it becomes an unconscious way of being. Even then, there will be times when you have to step back and be conscious again. Perhaps a specific situation presents itself to you for the first time. You might have intuitive ideas about how to handle it, but since you've never done it before, you must become more conscious to tweak your actions to the specific situation.

In the ballet of graceful leadership, the graceful leader pulls self back and others forward to do what is needed. When people talk about conscious leadership and servant leadership, they frequently talk about how the leader leads from behind. A leader who is always at the front, pulling their team along behind them, is not graceful. However, the humble, self-deprecating leader who is always at the back, out of the limelight, is not graceful either. A graceful leader recognizes that their role is fluid. Sometimes, yes, a leader needs to lead from behind. Other times, they need to be up front. The graceful leader can pull to the back in one moment and then march forward to the front in the next, intuiting what the situation dictates. They swing back and forth as needed, never staying in either position for one nanosecond longer than needed. In a crisis, they move up front, taking the hits and clearing the way, and then as soon as the storm breaks, they hand command off to their lieutenants and fall back, letting their team take over.

The graceful leader is focused on the collective, not on individual achievement. When my boss pulled me aside and told me I needed to change how I gave feedback, he was focusing on the collective. My individual achievement was high. However, it was more important that the team as a whole function smoothly.

Graceful leaders understand that the wins and losses are everybody's—theirs and their team's. Most leaders understand this cognitively, yet their behavior typically doesn't support that knowing. Too often leaders like to be up front when winning, taking credit. I'll have leaders tell me, "I got the metrics back, and I saved us 20 percent." I'll respond, "Oh, you did that by yourself?" Then they'll have an aha moment, because of course they didn't. Just as harmful are the leaders who disappear when winning. It's always "My team this" and "My team that" without acknowledging that the win is theirs as well. They think they're being humble when, often, what they're doing is depriving their team of sharing in a win. It's a balancing act that depends on each individual situation.

Adaptability underpins graceful leadership. It ensures situational appropriateness while remaining authentically you. You won't be the exact same leader to each person on your team, because each person requires different things. You could say something to one person, and they'll take it well, and to another person, the same thing will hurt their feelings. As a graceful leader, it is your responsibility to learn how to adapt your style and behavior without changing your foundational essence.

The graceful leader never forgets when they should lead and when they should submit to the leadership of the collective. Having moved from an "I" to a "we" construct, they intuitively and consciously understand that together a group of human beings with good leadership can come up with a more impactful solution than any one person can on their own.

I frequently see leaders go in with the attitude "I know how we're going to do this, and I'm going to guide them to my answer." That is manipulative, not graceful. Grace means letting go of the how and the outcome and actually letting the team come to their own solution. This doesn't mean the leader is passive. Rather, the leader is simply curious and open to all possibilities, withholding judgment. Think of a sailboat and how a captain charts a course. The captain sets a direction, then adjusts to the wind to harness its power to get to the desired location. Oftentimes it is helpful to picture yourself as the captain, guiding and harnessing the power of the team (the wind) to find the best course to the desired outcome. When you sense your need to control, pause, breathe, and be the captain. More often than not, the solution that arises from such co-creation is stronger than what the leader could come up with on their own.

From the outside, graceful leadership looks like gentle communication, curiosity, flexibility, and holistic problem-solving. It might look like a lot of work. From the inside, though, graceful leadership feels like an easy harmony, not work (once you get the hang of it).

MY FIRST EXPERIENCE BEING A GRACEFUL LEADER: GRACE IS BEING PRESENT

In 2011, I was brought in to coach Jeannie. Though upper management saw potential in her, she wasn't performing as well as they needed her to. In truth, Jeannie didn't have that much to work on. Accessing her self-awareness and learning some communication strategies looked to be the key to her moving the needle. This assessment sounds easy, and at some points in our development, it may be so; however, it's not always easy. While moving the needle one degree seems like a simple task, it can be challenging.

I sat down with Jeannie. As she explained the situation, she grew fidgety, and her tone became crisp. She felt her team was incompetent. Upper management was placing new demands on her, and she was struggling to meet them. No matter how she cajoled her team, they weren't getting the results they were supposed to. The whole situation was leading to overwhelming stress for her. She was having anxiety attacks and taking her stress out on her team, yelling and screaming in ways that were extremely inappropriate for a work environment. As she continued to share, her frustration shifted into tears.

In the past, I didn't have the time or patience for tears or excuses. Now, after all the alignment work between my head and my heart, I found myself seeing the her that was beneath the judgment, frustration, and tears. I simply stayed with her, let her have her experience, and remained present. This shift in how I showed up was unconscious for me; it was my new way of being. What used to be a very thoughtful and intentional thing for me in the beginning had become fully integrated into how I was in the world. The grace I had given to myself I was now giving to her, and it was transformative.

"Jeannie, tell me the feelings," I inquired gently.

Through her tears, she said, "I'm angry, frustrated...afraid."

That was interesting. It's not uncommon for people to experience fear at work. Jeannie's level of fear, however, didn't make sense for the situation. Yes, upper management was pushing her. They were also giving her the resources that she needed to succeed—they'd given her me, after all. Jeannie was capable of improving her performance, and her company was supporting her to that end, so why was she so afraid?

As we dug into that fear, she realized that it was coming from her childhood. When she was young, there were several male figures in her life who were less than lovely to her. Now, with her male boss putting his thumb on her and driving her to do better, those old feelings of fear were being triggered.

Once she realized that her fear was due to prior emotional baggage and not the current situation, she was able to adjust her behavior. Now, when stress came up, she would remind herself, "I'm not seven anymore. I'm thirty-one, and I have skills and competencies I didn't have then. I can handle this." In this way, she was able to upgrade her operating system and rewrite her story. She wasn't the scared little girl anymore, trying to please the male authority figures in her life. She was a powerful leader.

She learned to separate herself from her stress. Before, she *was* her stress. Now, she recognized that she wasn't stressed;

rather, she was *under stress*. Although she might be in an environment or in a moment that was extremely stressful, she didn't need to absorb and internalize all of that stress. The stress wasn't in control of the situation; she was.

She began to offer herself more grace, especially early on, before the stress became overwhelming. She learned to recognize her personal warning signs of stress, so that she could get in front of her stress and be the victor, not the victim. Days before her negative outward behavior—like screaming at her team—showed up, she would typically start drinking more in the evenings and exercising less. Once she identified those as early warning signs, she was able to recognize her stress sooner and take action to mitigate those feelings.

If I hadn't approached Jeannie with grace, we never would have gotten to the root of the problem. While she might have been able to alter her behavior in the short term, at some point, the same issues would have cropped back up. I feel almost certain that she would have been let go eventually. Instead, Jeannie was able to turn her entire professional life as a leader around, through a journey of self-discovery and acceptance that she was then able to extend to so many others in her life.

My coaching with Jeannie was a pivot point for me. From that moment on, I began working with grace more consciously. So many times in my coaching career, I've found that my clients mirror some of the same issues I'm work-ing with, whether it's on a micro or macro level. Jeannie was a giant neon sign reminding me that people show up differently than I do and are still amazing in their divine way. With years of practice, I can now suspend judgment within a nanosecond, and I'm only able to do that because of hundreds of people like Jeannie.

An integral reason I succeeded in being graceful with Jeannie was that I had become more conscious of my own tenden-cies and biases. Indeed, conscious leadership is an important step to graceful leadership.

THE MOVEMENT OF THE CONSCIOUS LEADER

In the United States, our companies are still very hierar-chical. We rely on leaders to make businesses work. So it's no surprise that leadership has long been a hot topic. The most recent evolution of the leadership discussion has led to the ideas of *servant leadership* and *conscious leadership*. Both concepts have value and serve as necessary building blocks toward becoming a graceful leader. You can't be a graceful leader without also being a conscious servant leader.

The servant leader understands the importance of leading from behind, offering support, and removing barriers. They understand that without the team, there is no leader. In the purest form, a servant leader is not self-sacrificing yet *is* in service to everyone—the people they lead, the community they serve, the clients they provide for. Servant leadership often leads into conscious leadership because serving others naturally leads one from an "I" construct to a "we" construct, which typically correlates with more conscious awareness.

The conscious leader is awake and knows who they are and are not. They know when to give and when to receive, and they understand the consequences of their actions. As a conscious leader, you bear witness to self and recognize that you are not your ego—that is, you understand that the voice speaking inside your head is not *you*; rather, it is a construct, a version of you that has been created over all the years of your life, with each new experience. This is a hard concept that triggers a lot of resistance. Most people's instinctive response is "What do you mean I'm not myself? Of course I'm me." As you become the observer of your experience, you can start to detach and understand that you are not the experience.

Being a conscious leader does not mean you're conscious in all things at all times. Rather, it means you understand when you are and are not conscious, and you take steps to create more consciousness. When you accept what is, you can be more present. When you become present and conscious, it gives you choice. And when you have choice, you can create change.

Reaching servant leadership or conscious leadership is an accomplishment in itself. It doesn't need to be the final step. Too many people get stuck at these levels, thinking they have unlocked their full potential as a leader. After servant leadership and conscious leadership, the next step is to evolve to graceful leadership.

Consciousness must evolve to a high level of complexity to meet the level of complexity of today's business challenges.
—Robert J. Anderson and William
A. Adams, *Mastering Leadership*

Conscious leadership is woven into graceful leadership. However, just because you are conscious and have a choice does not mean you always choose well. For instance, even if you see that you are not your ego, you may still choose to remain in your ego when you shouldn't. With graceful leadership, you extend your consciousness such that you become aligned with what you know to be right and true. When faced with the choice, graceful leaders are accountable to the laws of love and compassion. Their consistent alignment and realignment to the grace within them becomes a beacon for all of us to see, follow, and model, drawing us into grace as well.

Over a twenty-year period, using a variety of kinesiology tests and examinations, Dr. David Hawkins developed a classification system for levels of consciousness, from 0 to 1,000. The levels near the bottom of the scale, from 100 and below, include things like shame and fear. At level 200, we move into courage, which is the first move into consciousness. Half of the world is under 200. Love calibrates at 500. To raise your consciousness, you simply love all of life, from the beetle to the rushing river to the stranger on the street, understanding that we are all complete just as we are. 540 is where joy and gratitude reside. How we see the world is a direct reflection of where we are in our consciousness journey.

Map of Consciousness by David R. Hawkins (an excerpt)

LIFE VIEW	LEVEL	LOG		EMOTION
Is Perfect	Enlightenment	700–1000		Ineffable
	Peace	600		Bliss
Complete	Joy	540		Serenity
Benign	Love	500		Reverence
Meaningful	Reason	400	POWER	Understanding
Harmonious	Acceptance	350		Forgiveness
Hopeful	Willingness	310		Optimism
Satisfactory	Neutrality	250		Trust
Feasible	**Courage**	**200**		**Affirmation**
Demanding	Pride	175		Scorn
Antagonistic	Anger	150		Hate
Disappointing	Desire	125		Craving
Frightening	Fear	100	FORCE	Anxiety
Tragic	Grief	75		Regret
Hopeless	Apathy	50		Despair
Evil	Guilt	30		Blame
Miserable	Shame	20		Humiliation

For me personally, consciousness is an active exercise, a constant refining. I work at being conscious through meditation, nature practices, self-awareness exercises, and my gratitude practice. Grace can be experienced through various practices like these. It is a lovely by-product that one gets to witness and be a part of intermittently. Grace is bigger than just oneself. Consciousness is a practice, and grace is a being accessed through the practice. Essentially, graceful leadership is an evolution from the knowing of consciousness to the *being* of grace. When you step into graceful leadership, you move beyond awareness to actually living in alignment. It's like everything clicks into place and simply feels *right*.

TRANSCENDING CONSCIOUS LEADERSHIP: FALLING INTO GRACE

I was a conscious leader (not a perfect leader) for a long time—a decade and a half—before I began my journey into graceful leadership. I still have to work on being conscious because consciousness takes commitment and practice. Now, in addition to being conscious, I also have access to grace.

Conscious leaders are awake and understand the choices they have. Graceful leaders also understand their options, and they always choose the path of loving compassion. Truly, it is not even a conscious choice. They simply do it, because their grace is a way of being. They intuitively know which route to take. Conscious leaders, on the other hand, do not have to choose love and grace. Conscious leadership is an awareness, a way of *thinking*, whereas graceful leadership is a way of *being*.

To illustrate the difference between conscious and graceful leadership, let me tell you a story about a time I was conscious yet not graceful as a parent. My son was eighteen at the time. He and I have always been a lot alike, which brings unique challenges. At this point, he was making some not-great choices in his senior year of high school. These choices rubbed against my value system the wrong way, and I articulated this to him. Like most teenagers, though, he was content doing his own thing. At that point, I told him that I would not tolerate certain behaviors. If he chose to continue in the behaviors, the consequence would be that he could no longer live in my house.

Throughout this interaction, I was very conscious. I recognized that the reason I was upset was because he was acting in a way that was incongruent with my value system. Prior to becoming conscious, I would have just screamed and yelled. I wouldn't have tied it to my value system. I also probably would have said he was a bad person. Instead, being conscious, I was able to separate his behaviors from him as a person.

However, I wasn't graceful. I wasn't listening to all he was saying underneath the words or giving him the opportunity to convey his truth. I had already passed judgment, so there was no curiosity, no stillness, no openness to possibility. I approached him with a command-and-control mindset. I was mandating, not attempting to connect to his essence. Because of this, I was harsher in my words and fiercer in my action than I needed to be. Were this to happen now, I would do many of the same things. I would still start a conversation, and I would still be clear about the behaviors that clashed with my values. However, I would also act with more compassion and more respect for him as a person than I did.

Moving from consciousness to grace is about transitioning from self-awareness to an even more holistic "we" construct. With my son, I was conscious and aware of *my* self, not *his* self. The graceful leader recognizes that others' selves are just as important as one's own self, because the leader exists only in relationship to others. Leadership by definition requires others; followers and leaders are enlisted in a dance.

As leaders, it is our relationships with our followership that offer us the challenges and opportunities to refine ourselves into and through grace. Focusing on these relationships and your role in them will enable you to move fluidly from consciousness into grace. As an example, I recently got a call from a very stressed-out VP who was struggling with one of her team members. I told her, "This is the biggest gift you've been given. One of your goals was to learn to handle conflict better at work, and now you are smack dab in the middle of it. This person is going to refine you into the leader that you said you want to be."

The graceful leader takes a "do no harm" approach. This requires the consciousness of understanding that we are not our egos. The ego tends to be agenda driven. That's not a bad thing. You simply have to be aware of what your ego is doing and check it when appropriate. For instance, let's say my boss wants to see a 20 percent reduction in overhead costs in Q3. To make sure we can hit this number, I go to my team and tell them, "We need to get 30 percent cost reductions in Q2." I figure if they're striving for 30 percent, we will be able to hit 20 percent with no problems. Thirty percent might not be possible, though, and might put undue stress on my team. Because of my agenda, the reality gets muddled. I'm not clear and honest about my intention and might end up doing harm to them and my resources as a result.

Graceful leadership is an extension of conscious leadership. It does not require significantly more work or time. Rather than adding items to your to-do list, graceful leadership simply calls for a refinement of your way of being.

KEY TAKEAWAYS

Graceful leadership is a journey that begins with servant leadership and conscious leadership. While those forms of leadership focus on what you do and awareness of self, graceful leadership is about who you are being. When you continue past conscious leadership, grace becomes a state of being. To achieve this state, there are six tenets of graceful leadership that can assist you. These tenets are detailed in the next chapter.

FURTHER READING

- *Gene Keys*, by Richard Rudd
- *Power vs. Force*, by David Hawkins
- *Of Grief, Garlic and Gratitude*, by Kris Francoeur

CHAPTER 2

THE TENETS OF GRACEFUL LEADERSHIP

Along my journey as a leader of self and others and through my work as an executive coach to over a thousand amazing leaders, six tenets of graceful leadership have emerged. They include leading with and through *integrating, evolving, transparency, connecting, co-creating, and being compassionately powerful.* The journey into and with the tenets of a graceful leader is one of ebbs and flows. It is not a check-the-box, get-the-T-shirt activity. It is dynamic and will recede and expand with you in your own personal evolution as a leader. For those of us who like the satisfaction of completing something, this can be frustrating when first engaging. Once you have grasped the concepts and played with them for a while, the old sense of needing to accomplish something will diminish and be replaced with a new awareness and a new way of being.

INTEGRATING: MIND, BODY, AND SOUL

A leader skilled in integrating:

- knows and can communicate their own mission and vision/purpose;
- understands and is aware of internal body (health), as well as the messages their body language communicates, and manages both; and
- connects to a power larger than self, serving the collective goodness.

While the tenets are not meant to be chronological, I do believe that mastering the integrating tenet is foundational to finding success with the other tenets. Integrating your mind, body, and soul is the first step in bringing you closer to a single, unified *you*. Many of us develop more strongly in one area or another as we grow into young adults. For me it was my mind and intellect. What is it for you? Do you live in your body, head, or heart? When you're only paying attention to one or two of these aspects of yourself—mind, soul, or body—you will have an incomplete picture of *youness*. All three are needed to live a holistic version of yourself.

MISSION AND VISION/PURPOSE

Many people leave this lifetime never understanding that

they have a purpose, much less knowing what theirs is and then aligning their life to it. Do you know your vision/purpose? Can you state it in a sentence? In my experience, 90 percent of people can't. Nearly every company has a clearly written vision statement, yet as individuals, we don't take the time to craft and articulate a personal vision/purpose statement. Explicitly identifying your purpose is a gift to yourself. Having no statement or a vague idea leads to confusion and lack of clarity. With a proper vision statement, in one sentence, you tell the world who you are. A personal vision statement includes both *what* you do (your mission) and *why* you do it (your vision/purpose). (Hint: your vision/purpose statement isn't your job title; it speaks to your larger purpose: why you are here on this earth.)

> *Life is purposeful. Leadership is purposeful.*
> *A primary task of a life creatively led is*
> *to discern the purpose of our life.*
>
> —Robert J. Anderson and William
> A. Adams, *Mastering Leadership*

The process of digging and mining for your vision/purpose statement requires intention, commitment, and persistence. There is no rush in this process, as it is the process itself that holds the value. Unless you've already been thinking about this for some time, what you come up with in your first few attempts likely won't be *your* true vision statement. This is about integrating your mind and soul—defining your soul's innate purpose using words. This integration can be difficult, so this is something you must think about with focus and intention often over an extended period of time. In my case, I spent six years thinking, exploring, and refining my vision statement before I finally landed on my current version: I create safe spaces for souls to show up. That sentence sums up my truth, the core of who I am. It is my whole reason for being.

Your vision statement requires serious and playful thought, yet it needn't take you six years like it did for me. In fact, it is doable in just six months, if you stay focused and disciplined. So how do you go about creating your vision statement? I was asked this question so frequently by clients that I finally sat down and created a guided gratitude journal to lead people through the process. Upon completion of the journal, which can be finished in as little as six months, though many often take closer to a year, you get at least a paragraph version of your vision statement that you can keep refining all the time.

Your vision/purpose statement can and will evolve over time. If I'd crafted my vision statement when I was twenty or thirty, it would have looked very different. At this point in my life, I am pretty anchored on my vision statement. Another ten years from now, though, maybe my purpose will have morphed further.

In general, however, if you've managed to drill down to your core purpose, the why of your vision statement tends to stay fairly constant. What will change is the how. In my case, when I was younger, I created safe spaces for children. Then I did it through a recruiting practice and then through my coaching practice. Now I'm doing it through my writing and Ubuntu, my retreat center. While the purpose has expressed itself differently in my life, the root has stayed consistent.

INTERNAL AND EXTERNAL BODY LANGUAGE

Our bodies often speak to us. We don't always listen, though. For many years, my body was just the thing I used to get from the couch to the computer and to take the dog out for a walk. It was never a focus for me—until it stopped working the way it was supposed to.

I've suffered from Bell's palsy twice now, which is rare. Even rarer—and very fortunately—I recovered both times. It was my body's response to my working too much, not resting, and generally pushing myself past my limits for too long. The first time, I didn't know what was happening. The second time, I started to notice little changes and ways my body was warning me. Now, I can recognize my body's cues that I need to slow down. There's a feeling I get inside of my face that tells me, "Uh-oh, you're right on the edge." I didn't understand how to listen to my body before. You can bet that I listen to it now!

Some people are naturally more gifted at reading what their

bodies are telling them. If you're a thinker like me and spend most of your time in your head, you will need to make a conscious effort to work on listening to your body as well as your mind.

The first step is simply being awake to how your internal and external body language is communicating, and then you can work on interpreting and intuiting what those messages mean. Close your eyes and take inventory of your internal body health. Are your muscles tight? Is your gut calm? Do you feel alert or groggy and tired? Now what about your external body language? You can stand in front of a mirror for this one if you'd like. Are your shoulders tense, pulled up toward your ears? What kind of hand gestures do you use?

> *Our own physical body possesses a wisdom*
> *which we who inhabit the body lack.*
> —HENRY MILLER

For the most part, our bodies don't lie. There are, of course, exceptions, like when our bodies trigger fear responses that exceed what a situation calls for. However, compared to our minds, our bodies are more honest. Kinesiology is a testament to the body's inability to lie or be anything other than true, having an almost 100 percent accuracy reading every time. This makes our bodies a phenomenal tool in unlocking the truth. Our thoughts can cloud and overshadow our souls. If you're ever unsure about something, try listening to your body.

Remember that the ultimate goal is to integrate mind, body, and spirit. You don't want to listen to one to the exclusion of all else. In my experience, most of us spend the bulk of our time in our minds, so that's why I stress the importance of listening to your body, so that you can shift the balance. If your truth is that you are keenly aware of and living in your body, then you will instead focus on the mind and find experiences and resources to explore this part of the trinity that makes up you.

CONNECTION TO A POWER LARGER THAN SELF

Being a graceful leader requires connecting to a power larger than yourself that serves the collective goodness. You can call this power whatever you want: Source, Nature, God, Buddha, the Universe.

This power does not need to be religious in nature. It does, however, need to be for the betterment of everybody. Some people in society are connected to something bigger than themselves that does not serve the collective goodness. Typically, the thing they're connected to is rooted in hate or fear. We see this in xenophobia. When we honor anything that is not unity, we do not honor all that we are and our role in the collectedness. Connecting to a hateful or fearful power does not elevate one into grace. Rather, it pulls one down in limiting beliefs.

> *Discovering what allows our true selves to emerge is the secret to a magical life full of fulfillment and success. Serving others and expressing that service through our unique and important work is the secret.*
> —A. G. Lafley and Roger L. Martin, *Playing to Win*

Our grace center is directly plugged into Source, providing the access point to a higher power that serves the collective goodness. We are one with Source. When we are disconnected from our grace center, though, we resort to personal power, which is finite. Connecting to our grace center—and thus Source—strengthens us and allows us to tap into an unimaginable well of collective power.

EVOLVING: ALIGNMENT OF SOUL AND SELF

A leader strong in the evolving tenet:

- is relentless in the pursuit of understanding and aligning self to purpose;
- is a constant learner who is gentle in all pursuits, enlisting a lens of curiosity with a focus on integration; and
- creates relationships that have balance with giving and receiving and does both themselves.

In evolving, you stretch, test, and refine your sense of self, aligning it to your soul. In this book, I use *self* to mean the version of ourselves that is created by our ego based on our experiences in this life, while *soul* refers to our deeper, more innate self. (If this idea is foreign or confusing to you, don't worry—I go into much more detail about the distinction between soul and self and the alignment of the two in chapter 4, "Uniting Self and Soul.") In the process of aligning soul and self, you grow and become more firmly cemented in your identity as a graceful leader.

ALIGNMENT OF SELF TO PURPOSE

Once you have a definition of self—who you are—the next step is to figure out, "Is this self that I've created in alignment with my why for being on this earth?" If the answer is no (which it frequently is in the beginning), you must be relentless in pursuing alignment between self and purpose.

As you work to become a graceful leader, you will sometimes come across a gap between your belief system and your behaviors—a gap between your defined purpose in life and the things you're actually doing. Every time you find an incongruency like this, the work is in correcting the behavior to true up with the you that is emerging. Trust me, this is much easier to type on this page than to put into practice. I have found, as have many of the leaders I work with, that as soon as you find a gap and do the work required to create alignment, another gap is close behind. It is key here to remember to engage and be playful with this process. You are A-OK just the way you are; there is no better version of you that will end your evolution. It is the evolution itself that is the goal.

The joy of knowing your why is that it is a compass. Every single thing aligns to it, and if something doesn't align, you don't do that thing anymore. Perfection is not needed; your awareness and continued effort to seek alignment is all that is required. Several times, I have felt as if I was failing in creating this alignment, and the truth was I was trying to align to a "should," not something that was truly for and of me. Always return to your why—your purpose. It provides an incredible clarity to your life. I no longer have to worry about what I'm supposed to be doing, because I already know: I'm creating safe spaces for souls to show up. Whether it's creating an environment for others to lead more gracefully, building a retreat center, coaching one-on-one, or supporting my children, I know my purpose.

CONSTANT LEARNER

We're always growing—we're either learning or we're dying. The graceful leader embraces a mindset of constant learning. They are deeply curious, suspending all judgment.

It is remarkable what possibilities exist when you enlist a lens of curiosity. As has happened many times to many leaders, I was once given a set of goals for my team that seemed impossible to achieve. I initially felt quite a bit of resistance to the goals, feeling that my superiors had no comprehension of the reality as I knew it.

Nonetheless, that following Monday, I shared the goals with my team, working really hard not to share how stupid and unreasonable I thought they were. The next moment changed everything. A team member deployed curiosity about what it would take to reach these goals. His inquiry was received well by the others, and they began exploring how the team would need to work together if the goals were going to be reached.

Curiosity and stillness are closely connected. Although I was not as curious as I could have been, I presented the goals without projecting my judgments of them. I didn't have the purest intentions in holding back my thoughts about upper management and the goals. I simply wanted to push my team to achieve the goals even if I thought they were unreasonable. (Note: My grace wasn't as clean then as it is more often than not now; it was messy and gritty for a long while. In truth, in my most intimate relationships, the ones that refine me the most, there is still a great amount of grit. Graceful leadership is always a continual process.)

Regardless of my intentions, I created space for something else to show up—a new way, possibility, and solution. While I did not believe we could meet the goals, my team, by being curious, was open to that possibility. In the end, they were right. They not only met but exceeded the measures set out for us, and I couldn't have been more proud—not because they met the goals, but because of the way in which they did so.

I thought I knew everything I needed to know about those goals, but my team proved me wrong. The graceful leader is comfortable with the fact that they don't know everything, and they are open to relearning what they think they already know. They approach their learning with a focus on integration, so that the lessons learned do not fade out of memory and instead become a part of their life and being.

It is important to be gentle with both yourself and others in this pursuit of learning. There are peaks and valleys in life. The goal is to be a constant learner, yet 24/7, 365-days-a-year learning is not sustainable. Part of being graceful is being kind and gentle through any temporary setbacks.

BALANCE OF GIVING AND RECEIVING

A lot of people, including yours truly here, are really good at giving and atrocious at receiving. There is a humility in receiving, because there's a story hidden inside the act of receiving that suggests you need something that you can't give yourself, whether it be a physical item, a favor, or words of gratitude or praise. That is a vulnerable position, and it makes it difficult to accept gifts, much less ask for them.

If you feel overextended or like you're a victim to everyone else's needs, you likely have an imbalance tilted toward giving. This is hugely damaging on a personal basis. I see this issue a lot with mothers, who give, give, give to their children. Then their children move out, and they're lost. Without their identity of mother—endless giver of food, shelter, care, and love—they're left wondering, *Who am I?*

Such an imbalance of giving and receiving is detrimental to self and to those around you. For relationships and connections to exist and thrive, both giving and receiving have to happen. When you don't accept a gift, you are not receiving, and you are also taking away someone else's ability to give. Suppose someone notices that I might like a hug and offers me one. If I say no—despite everything inside of me screaming, "Yes!"—I am thwarting my heart's ability to receive what it needs. I am also preventing that person from experiencing the joy of giving and forming a deeper connection with me.

> *Start the spark of reciprocity by making requests as well as helping others. Help generously and without thought of return; but also ask often for what you need.*
> —Wayne and Cheryl Baker

Just as all giving with no receiving is damaging to self, so too is it harmful to only receive without giving. People with this trait tend to feel a sense of entitlement and can edge into narcissism. A one-way flow of receiving does not allow for the infinite circle of giving and receiving that is needed for healthy relationships. If you only receive, you withhold from yourself the great, rewarding joy that is to be found in giving to others.

Balance is the key. All receiving with no giving and all giving with no receiving are equally undesirable states. Neither is evolved, and neither makes way for graceful leadership.

TRANSPARENCY: SELF AND OTHERS

A leader with mastery of transparency:

- demonstrates authenticity in their behavior and communication (they walk their talk);
- is an active listener and is open, clear, and consistent with their message and its consequences; and
- doesn't base sense of self in labels or others' perceptions (they allow the people that follow them to see their heart, and they lead from this consciousness).

Transparency is about showing up to the world as yourself, no masks. It's important to achieve transparency with others and also within yourself. Note: Transparency is always situationally appropriate—know your audience.

AUTHENTICITY

You've likely met someone who says one thing and does another. Perhaps you've even been that person. I know I have been in the past. This incongruence between speech and action isn't necessarily about lying or lacking integrity. Rather, in many cases what we say is what we think we *should* be doing, even if it's not what we're actually doing.

Is there a gap between what you think you "should" do and what is really aligned with your calling, dreams, desires, and talents? Is there a gap between who you are and how you're behaving?

So often we take on the projections of what others (with all the best intentions) see us being and doing. It is here that listening to our bodies' signals can be life changing. I remember playing the clarinet all through school because I "should" learn an instrument. I would frequently get an upset stomach and feel overtired in the middle of the day. Later in life, I came to learn that these body signs are clues that I'm doing something that isn't congruent with my soul's purpose. Looking back, my stomachaches and tiredness make so much sense. It took me really tuning into my body twenty-five years later to make the connection between those body feelings and playing the clarinet. The more you practice authenticity, though, the easier it becomes.

Courage is the willingness to be authentic, to speak and act in ways that express and embody our vision of greatness. Authentic, courageous conversation is necessary for high performance.

—ROBERT J. ANDERSON AND WILLIAM A. ADAMS, *MASTERING LEADERSHIP*

Being authentic can be scary. As a small example, I hate wearing corporate clothing. (Don't get me started on pantyhose!) Even though I hate it, I did it for years and years. Only now, at fifty-one, have I stopped wearing corporate clothing. Sometimes I am somewhat concerned I'll get kicked out of corporate because I don't look like everyone else. Even though it makes me nervous to present myself differently from everyone around me, I do it anyway, because the clothes I wear now are much more authentic to me.

Fear is a natural response to vulnerability. You must be *courageously* authentic. Move forward despite fear, and remain true to yourself. In this way, you will begin to show up as yourself in all arenas of your life.

ACTIVE LISTENING AND CLEAR COMMUNICATION

You're likely already familiar with the idea of active listening in theory if not practice. When you are an active listener, you don't just hear the words being spoken; you listen to the message and meaning of the words. You then reflect that message back to the speaker in your own words to confirm your understanding. This requires you to be present in the conversation and offers the sender the opportunity to adjust their message to align with their intended outcome.

Graceful leadership requires clear, concise, candid communication. Mastering this kind of communication can be a challenge. A large part of my executive coaching practice is helping leaders refine the clarity and consistency of their communication. Good communication is key to being seen as a leader who knows who they are and where they're going, which inspires confidence and a sense of security in followers.

Remember that being a graceful leader does not mean being a doormat. You cannot shy away from difficult conversations. You must be firm and consistent in your messaging, and you need to enforce consequences when needed. In the words of Brené Brown, "Feeding people half truths or bullshit to make them feel better (which is almost always about making ourselves feel more comfortable) is unkind."[1]

SENSE OF SELF OUTSIDE OF LABELS AND OTHERS' PERCEPTION

Just because someone says you're something doesn't make you that thing. We all see others through our filters. When we share what we see and believe another to be, even when

[1] Brené Brown, *Dare to Lead* (New York: Random House, 2018), 48.

it is well intended, it comes through our filters. This is not good or bad—until we make it so.

Sometimes, when we see who we are inside and know it is not what is desired by others, we start the charade of creating a mask to wear so that others are more accepting of who we show up as. This behavior is damaging in the long run and takes a great deal of time to unravel, as we dismantle one mask at a time.

Grace requires that we develop a sense of self separate from others' perceptions. As such, awareness of who you are and what others project onto you is critical. Sometimes, though, it can be difficult to distinguish between the two, because others' perceptions worm their way into our minds, and we internalize them.

As an example, if you're the CEO, there's a perception you have of what a CEO looks and acts like. That perception could have formed for any variety of reasons—maybe it's based on movie portrayals of CEOs or an early mentor you had. Often there is a gap between your perception of what a CEO should be and what you actually are. This goes back to authenticity. If you try to force yourself to fit the image of what you think a CEO should be, there is a high probability that you aren't being authentic to yourself. The gap can widen even further if you try to mold yourself to fit others' expectations.

Letting go of labels and not worrying so much about others' perceptions allows you to be the CEO that you need to be to lead effectively. For instance, it used to be that CEOs were expected to dress the part. Now, many pay much less attention to clothing. They might buy seven pairs of the same pants and shirts, and they literally wear the same outfit every day. Though it may not fit with others' perceptions of what a CEO should look like, it allows them to be more comfortable and spend their time on more pressing issues.

There is no one right way to be a CEO or a VP or any other title or label you can think of. If you are a CEO, everything you do is what a CEO does. So let go of the labels and perceptions, and be the leader the situation calls you into being.

You get to decide who you are. However, it's important to remain aware of the external labels others place on you, as sometimes they can be indicators that your behavior is not aligned with your being. For example, if you know you are a caring person, but people around you see you as cold and distant, there may be a gap between who you are and how you act that you need to address. Other times, the issue may be in the label and the other people's perception. Whatever the case, when you feel and experience a discrepancy between your self and others' labels, it's key to stop and clear it up.

This part of your journey into grace can be bumpy and a bit messy. You may meet some resistance as people awaken to the shift you are creating. Oddly, for you, it will very often feel like coming home, more real than anything you have experienced, but it can feel very much the opposite for key people in your life. Some relationships and roles that are set up based on who others need you to be may fracture if who you truly are is not what they need you to be. This is simply an unavoidable side effect of growth. Every relationship is a dance both parties agree to (even if unknowingly), and if you change the steps to the dance, the other party may or may not choose to remain dancing with you. Whatever their decision, they are not right or wrong. The two of you may simply be in different places in your journeys. We are where we are, and there is no rush.

Grace plays a huge role here, as it affords you the opportunity to let others be where they are as you move on. When you experience someone projecting who they need or want you to be and you know that is not who you are, be curious and work to not be defensive. Be patient with others and yourself, as you are potentially redefining the who that you are in the world, and it will take time for everyone to adjust.

CONNECTING: SELF AND UNIVERSE

A leader proficient in the connecting tenet:

- has moved from the "I" construct of being to a "we" construct (the "we" is universal, not just humanity);
- has discovered and developed an inner guidance system that is connected to the collective; and
- demonstrates empathy and gratitude.

In the connecting tenet, you expand with grace beyond yourself and into the larger world.

"I" VS. "WE" CONSTRUCT

There is a term and philosophy from southern Africa that I love: *Ubuntu*, which means "You are, therefore I am." This is the core of the connecting tenet of graceful leadership. We are who we are because of each other.

Spend some time paying attention to how the people around you speak. Who tends to say, "I this, I that," and which people instead say, "We this, we that"? (Just notice the patterns, without passing judgment. As I'll discuss later, suspending judgment is a critical part of being a graceful leader.)

Even if we aren't aware of it, we live in a connected, collaborative world. Underneath every "I" is a "we," because none of us have made it to where we are in life without other people. I didn't get to be me all by myself. I had a whole lot of help. Now, whether or not I always wanted that "help" and whether it had a positive or negative impact on me, it did shape me.

As you step into graceful leadership, you become more aware of these connections, and you naturally move into more of a "we" construct. This "we" extends beyond humanity, to include animals, plants, our entire planet, and the whole of the universe beyond.

Note that shifting to this "we" construct does not erase personal accountability—the opposite, in fact. In understanding the ways we are all connected, we see the ways in which our personal actions have far-ranging impact beyond ourselves, making accountability all the more important. It's the butterfly effect—the idea that even the small actions you take today could somehow, someday, trigger a chain set of reactions that result in large effects.

INNER GUIDANCE SYSTEM

We all have an internal guidance system. Some call it the soul or the divine. Whatever you call it, this inner guidance system serves to guide us toward accomplishing our purpose. Since our purpose is connected to something larger than ourselves, so too is our inner guidance system connected to the collective.

Whether you recognize it or not, your inner guidance system

exists and influences your behavior, just like gravity. Your inner guide has always been there and is ready for your engagement at any time, ready to guide you into alignment. Your willingness to connect is all that is needed. How you do so may evolve over time as you grow more comfortable with and trusting of your inner guidance system. This is what I mean when I speak of "developing" your guide: you are not developing your guide itself; rather, you are developing the way you connect to and access it.

Most of us have an illusion that we control everything about ourselves. We believe that the brain is the power source of the human. The truth is that the heart center—where our inner guidance system resides—is the most powerful part of who we are. When we can connect our brains into our internal heart system, we activate our full power, taking advantage of all the resources we have as human beings. Doing this requires a suspension of control, and from personal experience, it's both terrifying and extremely empowering.

EMPATHY AND GRATITUDE

You cannot be graceful without empathy and gratitude. When you are empathetic, you witness and appreciate another's situation without picking it up and taking it with you. You do not try to own or dismiss their emotions; you simply behold them. You are present in the moment with that other individual.

Gratitude is being able to express appreciation in all kinds of different ways that are appropriate to a person, situation, or thing. Expression of gratitude is one of the clearest external signs of a graceful leader. In my opinion, gratitude is the door to grace. (For more on gratitude, see chapter 3, "Why Gratitude Is the Entry Point to Grace.")

CO-CREATING: INNOVATIVE

A leader who co-creates:
- seeks new ways of solving problems that are nontraditional to the way their profession/organization does;
- surrounds themselves with talent different from theirs and people competent in areas they are not; and
- demonstrates the ability to both lead and follow, all while maintaining the leadership role.

In co-creating, you learn to deploy other people's talents and resources instead of relying only on yourself.

NONTRADITIONAL PROBLEM-SOLVING

Graceful leaders are open to and actively seek out nontraditional methods of solving problems. What constitutes "nontraditional" will vary according to each individual, organization, and industry. The core idea is simply that if you always take the same route going home, you're willing and able to try a new route. You might not know whether that route will be better, yet you try it anyway.

In my experience, though leaders are theoretically open to new methods of problem-solving, they don't believe that it is possible in practice. I can't even count the number of times I've been told, "My organization would never support that" or "We don't have the resources for that." While that might be true, it doesn't stop the graceful leader from stepping back and looking at problems from a nontraditional perspective. Yes, it might not work out. You'll never know, though, if you don't at least allow the possibility.

DIVERSITY OF TALENTS

Graceful leaders attract and develop diverse teams, with a wide breadth and depth. The diversity of a team's strengths says a lot about the leader. Oftentimes, leaders will hire teams that look, act, and behave just like them. This is common when leaders have developed robust but one-dimensional networking groups along their career paths, as people are naturally attracted to and build relationships with those who are similar to them. These leaders frequently have gotten celebrated results with this approach, but they typically reach a point in their careers where they begin to realize that what got them where they are will not get them where they are going. Diversity at large is often what is required, and their teams are a great place to start.

The more varied perspectives you have, the more possibilities you open up to co-create in innovative ways.

ABILITY TO BE BOTH LEADER AND FOLLOWER

The graceful leader knows when to lead from the front, middle, or back of the team. They have a confidence in their leadership that allows them to feel secure in their position whether they are acting as leader or follower.

Think back to the infinity symbol from the introduction. At any moment in time, the graceful leader can be anywhere on the continuum inside that infinity symbol, and it's the perfect place for them at the perfect time. They are present in the moment and surrender to what the situation requires.

The beginning of this move into grace can be and can feel a bit scripted. It is. Over time you will integrate this new way of being into you and your leadership approach, and it will become as natural as breathing. As I typed these words to share with you, a big grin came across my face, as I have both traveled this path and guided so many other amazing souls along their own journey into gracefulness.

COMPASSIONATELY POWERFUL: IN ALL THINGS

A compassionately powerful leader:
- influences through an open heart and clear agenda, blending stillness and action;
- understands and owns the impact and consequences of their behavior to self/organization/world; and
- creates room for flow while maintaining structure.

In being compassionately powerful, the graceful leader is effective and achieves results without sacrificing people.

OPEN HEART AND CLEAR AGENDA—BLENDED STILLNESS AND ACTION

With work on the tenet of transparency, you will naturally begin to lead with a more open heart and a clear agenda. I like to joke that when I began to work on grace, just like the Grinch, my heart grew three sizes.

Part of what distinguishes a leader who is transparent with one who is both transparent and compassionately powerful is the blended stillness and action. We live in a "Go, go, go!" world of action. We plan out our days to the hour and sometimes minute, our calendars blocked out with meetings and to-do lists, overlooking the value in stillness. The compassionately powerful leader understands that there are times for action and times for stillness. They can work efficiently and effectively, yet they are also willing to stop and be present in the spaces in between. This kind of stillness allows space for empathy and gratitude and provides the silence needed to hear one's soul and tap into a higher power.

UNDERSTANDING AND OWNING THE IMPACT AND CONSEQUENCES OF ONE'S BEHAVIOR

The graceful leader understands and owns the impact and

consequences of their behavior. This one is pretty self-explanatory. A compassionately powerful leader does not blame others. They take responsibility for both the direct and indirect consequences of their behavior while also holding others accountable. For instance, if the team fails to meet its targets, the graceful leader owns their role in the situation while also holding the team accountable.

A signal that you are beginning to step into compassionate power is when you are able to hold the accountability for the team and yourself in a way that neither harms nor dismisses the consequences. This is also where a leader is able to practice resilience when unintended or unforeseen consequences show up. The ability to be still and assess the situation and determine the appropriate reaction is one that sits firmly in a leader's ability to be compassionately powerful.

FLOW WITHIN STRUCTURE

The compassionately powerful leader creates room for flow while maintaining structure. Leaders need to have a plan and a vision, sure. They need to know where they're going so that they can articulate it to others. At the same time, they need to be able to recognize when the structure they've created does not serve a particular situation or needs refinement.

When leaders are too rigid in their structure, they fail to notice opportunities for improvement. On the other hand, when leaders lack structure entirely, they spend resources ineffectively, wasting time, money, and energy while not getting any closer to the desired outcome.

A good example of this balance of structure and flow in action is how graceful leaders handle difficult conversations. They set their intentions and make their agenda clear to provide structure. Yet they also leave room for flow, because conversations should be two-way dialogues, not one-sided lectures. They let the conversation move to where it needs to go for the other person instead of running down the bullets on a list.

The compassionately powerful leader is like a river, with both structure and flow. The riverbanks channel the water's path along a set course, yet if a rock is dropped in the center of the river, the water can flow smoothly around it without hiccups. Graceful leaders are always looking forward, with a finger on the pulse of the situation. They can spot the ripples in the water that signify an obstacle is coming, and they adjust accordingly.

THE GRACEFUL TENETS IN ACTION: MICHAEL

Understanding the graceful tenets is easier when you can see them in action. Michael is an excellent example of what the tenets look like in practice.

Michael ran the whole operations division for a Fortune

500 transportation company. It was a high-stress, high-responsibility role, so to support Michael, his organization brought me in as a coach. Michael and I hit it off right away. As we worked together, he told me, "I'm a Christian man. I don't think people at work know that about me." He was frustrated by this inner knowing that who he said he was and how people were experiencing him weren't aligned. He felt a burning need to integrate his Christianity into his work life. He worried, though, about how he could do that without alienating his team, which was diverse, with a wide spread of religious beliefs.

This was my first clue that Michael was on his way to being a graceful leader. He had already begun work on the integrating tenet by connecting to a higher power—in his case, his Christian faith—and he also recognized a need for more authenticity, which is part of the transparency tenet.

It was an interesting challenge for us. How could he begin showing up as all of himself at work, Christianity included, while not crossing into inappropriate behavior? To reach a solution, he had to let go of the label "Christian" and define what it meant to him to be Christian in terms of behaviors. He decided that for him it meant showing up with compassion, listening, and being more still so people could express themselves.

As part of our coaching, we looked at some 360-degree feedback he'd gotten. The most poignant discovery was that his team wanted him to take more ownership and be more visibly there as their leader. They wanted him to get out of the back seat and into the driver's seat, and they wanted him to take credit for the wins as much as the losses. Whenever Michael was called to the front position for glory or credit, he was very uncomfortable. He had no desire for that kind of praise. This resulted in an imbalance of giving and receiving, indicating a need to work on the evolving tenet.

The conundrum was Michael's deep humility. He didn't know how to lead from the front while remaining a humble, Christian man. In his mind, they were dichotomies: he could be only one or the other. His team had made their desire clear, though, so we set to work. I asked him to compile a list of leaders who he felt led people effectively from the front while still being humble. Michael approached the process with an open mind and gentle curiosity, and slowly, he began to evolve.

In conjunction with this other work, I gave Michael a gratitude journal. Many of my clients are skeptical when they first start their gratitude journal, and Michael was no different. "Really?" he asked when I sent him his journal.

"Yes, really," I said. "You signed the contract. We're doing this."

Within the first month, his attitude had undergone a complete reversal. He even called me and asked for more journals so he could give them away to others.

From his journaling, Michael discovered that though he was *feeling* gratitude, in no way was he externally *expressing* his gratitude at the rate that he was experiencing it internally. Michael had all these gifts of gratitude that he was keeping inside of him instead of gifting to people. He committed to changing this. The next time he noticed his wife going through a hard time, he expressed his gratitude for her and all she did for their family by sending her flowers. He was specific and clear about why he was sending the flowers so that she could attach a positive emotion to the rough situation she was currently going through. He hadn't sent her flowers in a long time, and the gesture floored her, bringing tears of joy. Demonstrating gratitude is part of the connecting tenet, and by expressing more gratitude, Michael was able to become more connected with his family and his team at work.

Michael was making remarkable progress into graceful leadership. Then, Hurricane Harvey hit Houston hard, and Michael's new skills were put to the test in a major way.

Hurricane Harvey was an incredibly destructive storm. Many of the people who worked for Michael lost their homes and belongings. Since showing up with compassion was an integral part of being a Christian for Michael, that was what he did: he showed up with compassion in a big way.

His response to the storm also epitomized the connecting and co-creating tenets of graceful leadership. For the connecting tenet, he thought in terms of "we" instead of "I," and he acted according to his inner guidance system, demonstrating great empathy for his team. Together, he and his team raised money and got resources to the people who needed it. In regard to the co-creating tenet, he searched for and found innovative solutions to the hurricane's impact. Though it put him out of his comfort zone, he reached across departments in his organization to form subcommittees to support the company's employees in the wake of the hurricane. He also brought his wife into the relief efforts, because he didn't feel it was appropriate to have paid staff handling the logistics of the relief efforts when they themselves were in need of help. His wife took over that responsibility, orchestrating the delivery of meals and locating housing resources for people whose homes were now unlivable.

Michael had begun to blend his home and work lives in an appropriate way. He had stopped taking his work home with him as often, and now he was bringing his home into his work in the form of his wife's volunteer efforts. With his example, the culture of the organization began to shift. Other people started to get their spouses and families involved, and soon there was a whole network of community support.

Fast-forward a year, and Michael's staff nominated him for

a prestigious impact-in-leadership award. Only one person within the company won the award each year, and this year, Michael was that one person. He called me in a panic when he found out. He was supposed to fly out to attend a big ceremony to accept the award, and he didn't want to do it. He felt like he should send someone else to accept it on his behalf.

We sat together in silence, and he began to feel what was being asked of him. I gently reminded him that a graceful leader will move along the infinity circle as needed and pointed out that he was being asked to lead from the front in this situation. He reflected on what he remembered and believed about giving and receiving, including the importance of balance between the two. While he was the one receiving the award, it was just a formality so that he could bring it home and share it with the whole team. We both sat in a deep silence, one that connects all things and has a deep knowing. All the anxiety that he had felt when we'd first started this process had floated away with the tide. In this moment, all that he had set an intention to become as a leader was a part of him, and he felt it in every fiber of his being.

There is one tenet of graceful leadership I haven't mentioned yet: compassionately powerful. Michael is an interesting example of this tenet because he had to learn how to be compassionately powerful with himself, not just with others. Too often, the relationship we have with self is overlooked and undernourished. While it is easier to examine our external relationships, our relationship with self is the foundation for everything else. In Michael's case, he had to learn how to stand in his own power. When power is used lovingly and respectfully, it does not diminish one's followership; it actually elevates them. His team gave him a concrete example of this by nominating him for the leadership award and challenging him to see how his power and success could lift the entire team up.

RESISTANCE TO GRACE

Leaders often resist grace. The primary reason is there's a lack of awareness for the requirement of it. Servant leadership or conscious leadership is the goal, without the understanding that there are steps *beyond* that. As leaders, we simply don't hear the calling toward grace, or if we do, we hear it only intermittently in our lives. We may play with it for a minute, and then we put it away.

Even when we recognize the need for grace, we still resist it, seeing it as too inconvenient, too painful, too much work, and too risky, too unattainable. Those are valid concerns, and grace does not shy away from the difficult conversations, so let's talk about them.

THE INCONVENIENCE OF GRACE

Grace can feel terribly inconvenient. Sometimes it requires

sacrifices. As an example, I want to be a good steward of the land, and I also want a gas stove. However, if I have a gas stove, then that means I will be buying propane, and if I am buying propane, that means I'm supporting fracking, which, for me, is not being a good steward of the land. You see the dilemma? So now I have to learn how to use an induction stove, even though I would rather continue using a gas stove.

This example is a relatively small inconvenience. Even small inconveniences can add up, though. I use an app called Buycott that allows me to shop according to certain values—like women's rights, animal protection, and environmental issues. When I scan an item, the app lets me know whether that company is violating any of my core values. When I first started using the app, it was infuriating. I had to stop buying so many things. I wasn't angry at the app; rather, I was angry at the companies participating in business practices I found unethical. However, sitting with anger like that can be inconvenient, and fundamentally changing all my purchasing behavior has certainly been a challenge. It's worth it, though. The world will never change for the better if we don't change our individual behavior.

Embrace the inconvenience. Embrace the challenge. Doing the aligned thing is more important than doing the easy thing. The inconveniences will never go away. What will change is how you handle the challenges. Grace is a skill that you can build like any other. As you practice grace, you open up awareness of yourself and of everything. It's a constant refining, and it requires patience and practice.

THE PAIN OF GRACE

One of the challenges of grace is that it can dredge up negative emotions. Embrace those feelings, because that is a door to grace for yourself. When I stopped and looked at the fact that a lot of people were calling me a "bitch," it brought up shame and guilt. That told me that there was something there that was worth exploring.

To see a more conscious choice, we must become aware of the unconscious of our previous habit or tendency. This involves at least a moment of unflattering self-awareness, which usually feels uncomfortable.

—KEN WILBER, *INTEGRAL LIFE PRACTICE*

We tend to shy away from pain. Sometimes, though, we need to lean into the pain in order to heal, like the sharp sting of cleaning a wound. When we open up an inquiry—like when I analyzed why people called me a "bitch" and why that bothered me—we move into consciousness, which opens the possibility of grace.

This process requires vulnerability and courageous authenticity. If you are willing to be courageously authentic and work through these issues, you will find that the pain is temporary and diminishes over time. You will still rub up against sore spots from time to time. However, you will get more and more skilled at processing through those emotions with loving grace for yourself and the world at large.

THE WORK OF GRACE

Nearly every leader has felt the pressure of getting results at some point. Whether it's our boss, our shareholders, or the voice of our ego, we hear again and again the mantra of "Results, results, results!" When faced with this pressure, it's easy to dismiss grace as too time consuming or expensive.

"I don't have time for grace"—I hear this all the time, and I've said it myself just as many times. Struggling with an ever-expanding queue of to-do items, we forget to slow down and be present. At one point in my life, if one of my employees came to talk to me about their cat dying, I would have thought, *I don't care. All I care about is meeting our metrics.* As I became a more conscious leader and practiced more stillness, I realized that I actually *did* care about my employees' problems. However, I didn't know how I could both care and get results. How was I supposed to transition from "I'm really sorry about your cat" to "By the way, you still have to make your calls today"? Many leaders decide it's easier to simply drive for results and ignore everything else.

Being graceful *is* work. That work is worth it, because grace is not an obstacle to results; it is a path to them. It's like you have two different routes you can take to get to the store: one is a straight shot down a main thoroughfare with bumper-to-bumper traffic, and the other is a more winding path that avoids the cluster of downtown traffic. Though the straight shot might be shorter in distance, you're more likely to get into an accident or caught at traffic lights. While the other path is longer, the journey is more pleasant. And because there's no traffic, you typically arrive in about the same amount of time anyway. Which route would you choose?

The path of grace only *appears* to be less efficient. In reality, you can get the exact same results with grace that you get using command-and-control tactics, and the journey there will be much more pleasant. When you become skilled enough to hold someone highly accountable and love them compassionately through that accountability, amazing things happen. You elevate your team, raising them into whatever it is they need to be in order to be able to function at the level you're asking them to.

THE RISK OF GRACE

Often I work with leaders who *want* to lead with more grace yet think it's too risky for their work environment. While many leaders feel in their gut that they need to be more present, kind, and inquiring, they're told, sometimes explicitly and sometimes implicitly, by the business to *not* do that. "HR says I don't have a right to ask about someone's personal life," clients tell me. "So when I notice a change in someone's behavior, what am I supposed to do beyond asking why they're not meeting their metrics?" Too many companies are built on inconsistent and unclear cultures, so this is a real challenge. (However, the more people lead with grace, the more company cultures will change; see chapter 7, "How Grace Can Transform a Company's Culture.") The solution is to not poke and pry and rather to create space for the other person to come into. Sometimes they will open up, and sometimes they won't. As the leader, your job is simply to set the groundwork for the possibility and then accept whatever the outcome is.

Some leaders also worry that expressing more gratitude will cause people to take advantage of them. "I've been giving gratitude, and now everyone wants a raise!" one client told me, throwing up her hands. Her efforts to express more gratitude seemed to have backfired. She'd gone from 0 to 100 on the gratitude scale, and it confused her team. They didn't understand how she could be complimenting them so much and still giving them low review scores.

When clients are worried about giving too much gratitude, the first thing I ask them is, "Are you giving gratitude or recognition?" Gratitude is appreciation of any kind, and recognition is praise for a job well done. You can express gratitude with no recognition: for example, "Thank you for being compassionate when Jennifer needed someone to talk to. I really appreciate you taking the time to do that." Recognition, on the other hand, implies that the person is performing their job well: "Thanks for getting that report out early," "Thanks for closing that big sale," "Thanks for helping the client solve their problem." Giving recognition is important, *when it's warranted*. There are other ways for you to express gratitude without tying it to recognition.

As with all new skills and behaviors, it helps to be careful about going from 0 to 100. Expressing and living in gratitude is no different. Personally, I think that whenever you create a change, the first step is articulating it. If you are picking up a gratitude practice, it's as simple as telling your team, "Hey, I'm working on expressing more appreciation, so if you notice something new or different, that's what's going on." Or if that's not your style, you can ease into the gratitude practice, giving it a spin once a week at first. Then, based on the response, you can provide more clarity if needed or simply increase the frequency.

If after this you still have employees asking for raises or better hours or favors of some kind, have a candid conversation about it. Explain to them, "Not all gratitude comes with a dollar value attached. However, all gratitude comes with the deep feeling of gratefulness to you, and that's what I'm expressing." Most people will understand this reasoning.

As with anything worth doing, there are risks with grace. As Jessie Woodrow Wilson Sayre said, "To push oneself to one's limits inevitably involves risk, otherwise they wouldn't be one's limits. This is not to say that you deliberately try something which you know you cannot do. But you do deliberately try something which you are not sure you can do."[2]

THE CASE FOR GRACE

When leaders tell me that grace is too time consuming or expensive to implement, I say, "I hear you—tell me, how did you get to that belief system?" This conversation tends to go in one of a few ways.

Usually, they start explaining how busy they are. They see graceful leadership as an activity—another thing they have to do. In reality, graceful leadership is a way of being. It doesn't require extra time. Now, being a conscious leader *does* take some time. Gracefulness is an outcome of consciousness, so it does not take any extra time. It's simply who you evolve into. So if someone says they don't have time to be a graceful leader, what they're really saying is that they don't have time to be the best version of themselves.

Other times, this conversation leads into deep emotional discussion, sometimes reaching back to childhood. This is

---

2   Frederic Laloux, *Reinventing Organizations: A Guide to Creating Organizations Inspired by the Next Stage of Human Consciousness* (n.c.: Nelson Parker, 2014), 49.

an exciting transformational space to be in. It's a privilege for me to be present as people become curious about their beliefs and question whether those beliefs are serving them anymore. Who you are now is not the same person you were ten, twenty, or however many years ago. You don't need the same operating system you used when you were a kid. That system is outdated and needs to be upgraded to fit who you are now.

Our belief systems are often linked to our generational upbringing. Younger generations coming into the work-force—like millennials and Generation Z—are typically more open to self-awareness and consciousness work than older generations. Studies show that if you want to recruit individuals from these younger generations, you'd better be able to tell them what the purpose of the work is. Younger people tend to be more keenly aware of their value systems and work to align themselves accordingly.

This has created an interesting paradigm shift and a challenging workplace. We now have fifty-year-olds who don't understand their purpose leading millennials, for whom purpose is deeply important. If a millennial approaches a baby boomer and says that they want to live a purpose-driven life and that their purpose is to impact women's rights across the globe, the baby boomer might think, *Well, that's the stupidest thing ever.* So it's no surprise that conflicts can occur between people of different generations.

If you feel resistance to the idea of grace, get curious about what kind of impact you could have as a graceful leader. Besides curiosity, to cultivate grace, your greatest tool is gratitude. In the next chapter, we will explore how to activate your gratitude muscles and why.

FURTHER READING

- *Dare to Lead*, by Brené Brown
- *Reinventing Organizations*, by Frederic Laloux
- *Integral Life Practice*, by Ken Wilber, Terry Patten, Adam Leonard, and Marco Morelli

CHAPTER 3

WHY GRATITUDE IS THE ENTRY POINT TO GRACE

There's a problem that sabotages most leaders: a perpetual focus on what *isn't* working in their organizations, their relationships, and within themselves. Cultivating gratitude will help you shift your focus and see and appreciate all that *is* working in the many facets of your life. This appreciation leads to more flexibility and actually makes it easier to fix those things that aren't working.

INTELLECT ISN'T ENOUGH; YOU NEED HEART

Being smart isn't enough. This is a difficult truth to accept, because so many of us excel in our careers based on the strength of our minds. We don't connect to others through intellect, though. We connect through the heart. For this reason, executing excellence will only take you so far.

Kal, a surgeon at a prominent hospital, is a good example of this. Kal has undoubtedly achieved a mastery of surgical skills. He is good at his job, and he knows it. Recently, though, he's been dealing with complaints from people who work with him. Frustrated, he told me, "You've got to be kidding me! We're in the OR. All I should have to worry about is saving a life. I shouldn't have to worry about hurting a nurse's feelings or speaking abruptly or dropping the F-bomb if I need to." Kal's frustration is understandable. It's difficult to feel like you're performing your job well and it's still not enough: you have to do even more, not because of yourself but because of *other people*.

To become a leader, you typically must shift from an executing function to influencing role. You're no longer executing the skills you have mastery of and instead influencing others to execute those skills. This change is not always intuitive. When I realized that being a top performer wasn't enough and that I had to learn new skills to be a leader, I was sad and, honestly, angry. I'd spent my entire life focusing on developing my intellect and negotiating skills. It felt like I'd spent years building this soaring tower, and now I had to knock it down and start all over, right when it felt like I'd finally finished building. (In reality, I didn't have to completely knock my tower down; I just had to do some major renovations on it.) I wanted people to just do their jobs and stop whining. My attitude was "Are they doing the job or not doing the job? If they're not doing the job, kick their ass into gear. If they are doing the job, pay them for it." It was that simple.

Changing this attitude required accepting that the change was needed and beneficial. It took me a fair amount of time to undo all my prior programming and accept that caring and connecting *mattered*. Gratitude was my door to that fundamental shift.

Gratitude gives you access to other parts of your being than intellect does. It is a way to connect to heart, both within yourself and with others. The more you appreciate people, the more you're willing to adapt your leadership style in order to best lead them.

CULTIVATING GRACE THROUGH GRATITUDE

I first began to see grace on a regular basis when I implemented gratitude practices into my coaching. Gratitude is proven to work. There is science behind it. (See the resources at the end of this chapter.)

As an example of the power of gratitude, I had one client who scored 288 on her initial social and emotional intelligence assessment. This score was in the mediocre range. As part of tracking her growth, she wanted to get that score over 300, which would be just above average. She started a gratitude practice, and five and a half months later, she retook the assessment and scored 326, which moved her into the strong range. She credited her gratitude practice with the improvement. The shift in her perspective enabled her to tackle existing problems in new ways, removing barriers that had been there for years.

Most of us don't pause to appreciate ourselves and others. The only times we pat ourselves on the back are when we achieve large goals, like getting a promotion or winning an award. What about the smaller moments, though? What about the time when you needed to have a tough conversation with someone and you both managed to come out of it feeling good instead of misunderstood or thrown under the bus?

When I began asking my clients to slow down and tell me about their high-five moments—things they were proud of—they started to show themselves more grace. They stopped looking at only the things they did wrong and started also seeing what they did well. This reflection is a calibration. Just this week, I did this while talking with one of my clients on the phone. From the tone of her greeting, I immediately knew something was wrong. "Okay, what's the challenge?" I asked. She downloaded the entire challenge, and then right behind it, I asked, "Okay, and what are two of your high-fives from this week?" The high-fives put the challenge in perspective and created balance. Gratitude reminds us that our challenges are usually not as big as we think they are. And when we feel overwhelmed, our gratitude practice offers us solace—a place to be and find resilience when we do not think we can make it through the challenge presented.

Gratitude helps us be more graceful with others as well as ourselves. As leaders, we often tell ourselves the story that our team members are creating issues for us. When we stop to appreciate what they do well, we can move away from that story. (For more on how to step outside of story, see chapter 5, "Use Grace to Distinguish Story from Fact.") With gratitude, we approach our team with gentler communication and more flexibility. We begin to lead in a collaborative as opposed to command-and-control, manipulative, or dictatorial way. We enter into more integrated, holistic problem-solving that addresses the root problem, not just the problem that presents. This is key, because most of the time, the problem that presents isn't the real issue; it's simply a symptom of the true problem.

> *Gratitude is not only the greatest of all*
> *virtues, but the parent of all others.*
> —CICERO

Our wiring makes us assess our world quickly, which has

great value. Judgment in and of itself is not good or bad. It is how we apply judgment and assign meaning to it that can create mischief. Becoming aware of our judgments and learning to suspend them at will when needed allows us to connect to others.

Cultivating gratitude helps build this awareness. A few months into a gratitude program, I hear my clients' language change. The more gratitude they express, the more compassionate they become, both with themselves and with others. They learn things about themselves that they may not have realized before. For instance, I personally didn't realize how important nature was to me until I looked back through my gratitude journal and saw it come up time and time again. With a more compassionate lens, you become more curious, about yourself and the world around you. Curiosity inherently decreases judgment. At the peaks of your gratitude practice, as you look for appreciation in everything, you'll sense almost every nuance of judgment that you're placing on yourself, your world, and the people around you.

Gratitude is the catalyst—the door to curiosity, suspension of judgment, and, ultimately, grace.

THE POWER OF CONNECTING THROUGH THE HEART IN THE WORKPLACE

Some of my clients accept that gratitude allows you to connect to the heart, yet they don't understand why they need to connect to the heart in the first place. I like to tell them the story about the time I had to assist in downsizing a newspaper's entire staff.

I spent a lot of my career in recruiting, so I worked a lot with HR professionals. I often found HR frustrating. As a recruiter, I was playing offense, trying to deploy the right talent in the right place at the right time for optimal results. In contrast, HR plays defense, setting up systems and barriers with the intention of protection. Their purpose is to make sure no harm is done to the organization or the organization's people. As a result, it often felt like HR was in my way, preventing me from winning.

When my heart started to open up, I moved away from judging HR to being curious, asking, "Why are they 'in my way'?" I came to understand that many people enter HR with the best of intentions. They start with heart and want to help people; however, the systems in place don't always allow that. A perfect example is HR-speak when it comes to downsizing: "We have to let thirty-two people go, but it's best for everyone" or "This isn't personal." Downsizing is never pleasant. HR-speak like this makes it worse, though, in my opinion. This kind of language fails to acknowledge the damage that's being done. Downsizing is *not* best for everyone. It's definitely not best for the thirty-two people losing their jobs. And *of course* it's personal. I don't know of many more personal things than taking away someone's paycheck and livelihood. However, part of HR's job is to protect the company, so there are specific things they can and cannot say. It's a conundrum.

When I was working for the *Houston Chronicle*, one of our sister papers in Seattle was closing down. I flew out there as part of a team to release everyone due to it closing. I was on new ground. I was used to hiring top talent, not letting it go. As a result, I wasn't hardened to the process and was feeling it as if it were my own career ending in many ways. There's a false belief these days that we can't be seen as compassionate and loving when layoffs are necessary. It's linked back to HR's need to protect the company from legal liability. I wasn't part of HR, though—I didn't know the HR rules, much less care about them. So I handled the process differently. On the plane ride over, I actually prayed that I would find the kindest words and the best way of being with these people in order to preserve the greatest dignity for them in this really tough time.

I'd been working on connecting to heart and stepping into grace, and this role was when I first began to apply what I was learning. I'd fired people in the corporate BS way once before, and I knew that didn't have any heart. So this time, I tried to be present with each person for however long they needed. I acknowledged how hard this situation was for them. Losing a job is just that: a *loss*. There is a grieving process with it just like there is with any other loss. Part of grieving is letting go. One way to let go is to tell your story. Once you tell your story, you can close that chapter of your life and start writing the next one. We'd been given binders with a script and a checklist to complete. Nowhere in that checklist did it say, "Ask about their story and listen to it." I did it anyway.

Some people let me have it. I didn't judge their anger or hurt. If somebody needed to scream at me about what a piece of shit the company was, then I just listened. I didn't defend or agree; I just met them where they were. I let the situation be what it was, without forcing it to be something else or feeding it. When you lead from grace, you are no longer restricted by duality. It's not a question of protecting the person *or* the company. You can allow the person their dignity without throwing the company under the bus, and you can maintain the company's integrity without disrespecting the person.

My approach made a difference. One man grabbed my hand and thanked me. "You're here with me heart to heart, not just giving me bullshit," he said. I got a lot of hugs. One person contacted me afterward on LinkedIn to thank me for the kindness I showed.

Each of us on the downsizing team had twenty to thirty people we had to let go. Despite my different approach, it didn't take me any longer to finish than the other people on the team. The idea that allowing time to listen and be present takes hours longer is an illusion. When you let someone be where they need to be, you reduce the friction; you reduce the fight.

Since it didn't take significantly more time, why *wouldn't* I take the more heartfelt approach? The expressions of gratitude made it clear that doing so made a big difference to the people being fired. As if that wasn't already clear enough, I was about to get a firsthand lesson. When I returned from Seattle, I lost *my* job. I was completely blindsided by it. No one listened to my story, not one person, and I wanted that so desperately. It reinforced to me the importance of heart in the workplace.

> *[Leaders] need to be in touch with their*
> *hearts as well as their heads.*
>
> —LEE G. BOLMAN AND TERRENCE E.
> DEAL, *REFRAMING ORGANIZATIONS*

It can be scary to keep your heart center open through difficult conversations filled with conflict, fear, and anger. We are afraid of being hurt, so negative feelings tend to make us close off to protect ourselves. However, it is exactly when someone is experiencing those emotions that they most need love. The biggest compliments I've ever received are when employees tell me that I bring them in and ask them to leave with the same love.

The heart is the center of our feeling intelligence, our intuition of Spirit, and our capacity to love and care for ourselves and others. A conscious, healthy, strong, and open heart enables us to breathe freely, feelingly, and fully—and to commune with our source and purpose and with others.

—KEN WILBER, *INTEGRAL LIFE PRACTICE*

Results fade away. We don't remember that one month ten years ago when we hit our metrics. We remember the people who had a lasting impact on us. As cited in Tom Rath's *Strengths Based Leadership*, when followers were asked about times leaders contributed to their lives, they frequently used words like "caring, friendship, happiness, and *love*."[4] If you want to have the greatest influence on the people you lead, connecting through the heart is the way to do it.

COMPASSIONATE VS. NICE

Connecting through the heart center is about being compassionate, not nice. Nice is one-dimensional, and compassionate is multidimensional. When you're being compassionate, you actually feel it, and so does the person receiving the compassion. Compassion requires connection. When you're just being nice, it's superficial. You might enjoy being nice, and it can feel pleasant when someone is nice to you, yet there's no deep resonance of connection.

4   Tom Rath, *Strengths Based Leadership* (New York: Gallup Press, 2008), 85, emphasis mine.

Being nice is about preserving comfort and keeping the status quo. Niceness may or may not be true. I'm sure you can think about times in your life when you plastered on a fake smile just to keep the peace. Compassion, on the other hand, is always true. Though compassion is for the greater good, it might be uncomfortable. When you're nice, you try to smooth things over in the short term, sweeping problems under the rug; when you're compassionate, you understand that addressing issues as they arise is a heart-centered, loving act, though that does not always equal easy.

According to Monica C. Worline and Jane E. Dutton in *Awakening Compassion at Work*, there are four parts to compassion: attention, interpretation of the suffering, the felt empathetic concern, and an action to alleviate the suffering. Nice usually focuses just on the first step of attention and sometimes involves moving to action. When you're being nice, you may jump to fixing the problem that presents without first being still and *understanding the problem that is present*.

To understand this distinction, imagine that an employee tells you their house burned down. If you're being nice, you will give attention to the problem—"Oh, that's terrible!"—and then maybe you'll jump to the solution: "Let me help you find a new house." If you're being compassionate, you will sit with the problem longer. You will *interpret* the suffering and have empathetic concern. A lot of people have boundary issues with empathy. If your employee's house burned down, you don't need to feel as if your *own* house burned down, because it didn't. You want to try to feel what your employee is feeling in that situation, not what *you* would feel in that situation. It's a subtle distinction that can help keep you from taking ownership of too much emotional weight from others.

If you take the time to be compassionate in this scenario, you might realize that what your employee really needs right now is *not* a new house. There are a whole host of challenges to face when you lose a home; the house itself is just one. Your employee might need medical care or clothing, or they might be struggling with grief over the loss of treasured keepsakes. If you are nice instead of compassionate, you might step over your employee's true needs in your focus on the most obvious problem. Engaging compassion results in more holistic problem-solving.

There is a place for both niceness and compassion. However, nice as a *replacement* for compassion is a mess waiting to happen. If you're nice by default, you pay the cost in the form of tolerating bad behavior. The more nice people are on the surface, the more passive an organization becomes, whether it presents as passive-aggressiveness or apathy. Nice is a way to prevent disruption, to avoid the truth, to move quickly through a conversation, to placate. As a result, nice organizations tend to struggle with properly managing conflict and enacting change. Conflict simmers below the veneer of nice, and people feel as if they can't impact anything, for fear of not being nice.

Nice organizations tend to overcommit and underdeliver. They're unwilling to say that they can't do something, so they quickly become overextended. Andrew, one of the most amazing leaders I know, struggled with this issue. He worked for an aerospace company, and they were having a major issue with a vendor that was resulting in a $3 million loss. He kept checking in with the vendor to ask whether everything was on time, and the vendor always said yes. He couldn't understand how issues were happening.

"And you accept that yes answer, even though the results don't support it?" I asked. "You're not digging in and asking more questions?"

"No. They said yes."

"Well, you're just being nice. It sounds like they're not telling you the truth."

"Why wouldn't they tell me the truth?"

"I don't know. Why wouldn't they?"

"I really don't know. If they just told me the truth, we could probably fix whatever's wrong."

"Do you tolerate things needing to be fixed?"

He thought for a moment and then said, "Not really."

"So why would they come to you?"

He nodded in understanding. "I see what you're saying."

Andrew was rewarding nice behavior without realizing it. Being nice is a great trait to have. The issue is when you are rewarding niceness at the expense of something else, like accountability or the truth of a situation. This $3 million mistake could have been avoided if people weren't so nice. The employees were being nice to cover up issues, and Andrew was being nice instead of confronting the problem. As a leader, you need to create the safety for your employees to not be nice, which means being able to ask for help without worry of reprimand and negative consequences and being able to tell you when you're wrong and your ideas won't work.

Andrew stopped being nice and was compassionate instead. While he was never terribly punitive or a yeller, he also hadn't created the landscape that mistakes could be talked about, learned from, and maybe capitalized on. He'd always given off a perfectionist vibe, so he started having vulnerable conversations in which he expressed some of the mistakes he'd made before. Everything started to change. The vendor's issues preventing the parts from being delivered on time were identified and addressed, and in general, his employees felt more comfortable bringing problems to him.

Getting in touch with gratitude can help you become more compassionate because gratitude stretches your curiosity muscles. As you grow more curious, if you're hearing "Yes" all the time, you might start to ask more probing questions to determine whether that "Yes" is true. You start to understand that your team might have good reasons for not performing, and so you offer them more compassion, which creates the space for them to let down the facade of nice and allow what is true and real to come forward.

BUILDING A PERSONAL GRATITUDE PRACTICE

Though the benefits of gratitude are well supported, cultivating gratitude can be tricky. It requires a shift in mindset. One of the methods many people have had success with is journaling. So when I first began my coaching practice, I would gift my clients with a beautiful leather journal. The cover was buttery soft and the pages luxuriously thick. And the smell! The smell was heavenly. I was so excited about the journals. *Everyone's going to love this! Who wouldn't want to journal with this beautiful book?* I thought. Well, my clients used the journals all right—to write their to-do lists.

I was frustrated, and so were they. Many of them didn't want to be journaling in the first place. They were high-level corporate executives, and some days they didn't have time to eat breakfast let alone journal. Plus, they didn't understand *how* to journal, and why would they? They'd never done it before. Since they had no framework, the idea of journaling was overwhelming.

After several experiences like this, I created my first guided gratitude journal. It's a simple, gentle guide—something to provide direction. With this guide, my clients were much more successful in consistently completing their gratitude practice, weaving it into their lives. They simply needed a structure to help them get started. Then, usually about halfway through the journal, they were able to start adapting and creating their own personal gratitude practice. They would take some parts of my guide and ignore others, making their gratitude practice their own. This is always an exciting time, as it means their gratitude practice will stick and evolve as they do.

My clients appreciated my first journal so much that I created a second one and am currently designing a third. The first journal is focused on helping you connect to yourself. The second journal is about working on the connection between you and the world, with the goal of crafting a personal vision/purpose statement by the end of the journal. The third journal will be about refining yourself through relationships. The journals can be completed in any order, depending on what you want to work on first.

A gratitude practice is simply about feeling and expressing gratitude for things in your life. Each person's gratitude practice tends to look a little bit different. The key is to find something that works for you. In case you're feeling completely lost, I will share with you the structure of my gratitude journals. I've had great personal success with these journals, and they have been a solid foundation for my clients to work from. Try this framework out and feel free to adapt it in whatever way feels right to you. (You can follow along with this framework in any blank journal. If you would prefer to have a copy of my designed gratitude journals, they are available at my website store, www.alexsysthompson.com/store.)

The journals are designed to be used in the morning and at night. In the morning, you start with a quote, pieces of gratitude, an intention for the day, and supporting behaviors for your intention. At night, you do a wrap-up, where you list a high-five to yourself, magical moments of your day, and the intention you want to take into sleep with you. Consistency matters here. Try to work on your gratitude practice at least once a day. Don't beat yourself up, though, if you miss days here and there—it happens to all of us.

I start each page of the journal with a quote because it's a good way to get thinking and to look at the world through a different lens. If you're working from a blank journal, there are lots of great quote-a-day email, website, or app tools you can use.

The next section is for listing one to three things you're grateful for. Some days, you might have thirty different pieces of gratitude rolling off your tongue. Other days will be more of a struggle. Maybe all you have to be grateful for is that you got up out of bed. Just be sure to write *something* down. I suggest doing this as early in the day as possible, while you're still in bed even or while you're having your morning cup of coffee. Doing this early makes sure you're starting your day with an attitude of gratitude.

Next, you set your intention for the day. This is just one word or a short phrase. Some intention words/phrases I've used are "accepting," "don't be a shithead" (for those days when I wake up on the wrong side of the bed), and "curiosity." You want to keep this short so that it's easy to hold on to it throughout the day. If you write a long sentence, you're not as likely to remember it. When I first started doing this, I would write my word on three different sticky notes; I would put one on my bathroom mirror, one in my car, and one on my computer. It was easier for me to focus on my intention when it was physically in front of me throughout the day. Some of my clients have had success with setting periodic phone alarms or using apps to remind them to come back to their intention. If you find yourself struggling to hold on to your intention, set up some system of reminders for yourself. Note that you do *not* need to choose a different intention word every day. You can have the same word for however long you need it.

After setting your intention, you identify supporting behaviors. This is very important to help ensure that your intention translates into actions. If you don't articulate supporting behaviors, you'll miss the mark. If my intention is to not be a jerk, one of my supporting behaviors is often "I will edit myself before I start speaking without compassion." If my intention is curiosity, supporting behaviors could be "If I get frustrated with someone's behavior, I will ask myself why they are acting that way" or "I will find out one new thing about one of my employees."

At the end of the day, you come back to the journal and list a high-five to yourself. This is where you celebrate your wins—anything that you did well or that you're proud of. You can think of it as gratitude for self. These don't need to be huge accomplishments. Part of a gratitude practice is learning to be grateful for the small things. Sometimes my high-five is as simple as finishing my to-do list or taking the time to do yoga. If you don't pause to give yourself a mental pat on the back for these little things, they'll pass without notice.

The magical moments section is for moments, people, or experiences that added value to your day. This is a place for your gratitude for others. My dog frequently makes it into my magical moments section for her infectious joy. Some of my clients like to write down their magical moments as soon as they happen to help them feel the gratitude in the moment.

The last section is the intention you'd like to take into sleep with you. This intention can be longer than your daily intention. I tend to write a couple of sentences for it. To pick this intention, think about a problem you're wrestling with or anything that has been nagging at you. You'd be surprised at how many "problems" you can resolve while asleep simply by setting the intention. I personally find it most helpful to actually write this intention down, while some of my clients prefer to just think about it before bed. To each their own!

Next to these structured sections, I leave a decent amount of blank space for "margin madness." This area is for you to use in whatever way you would like. You could jot down words or phrases or doodle.

Throughout my journals, about once each month, I include extra challenges for the user to complete. Depending on the specific journal, this could be expressing gratitude to people in your life, doing an assessment to learn more about yourself, or going back and analyzing your journal entries for patterns. Once you get comfortable in your personal gratitude practice, try setting challenges for yourself to stretch your gratitude muscles further. It's typically easiest to start expressing gratitude in a private way, like in a journal. The ultimate goal, though, is to be able to express that gratitude externally as well.

HOW A GRATITUDE PRACTICE CHANGES YOU

When you start a gratitude practice, you start noticing more things to be grateful for. It's like the Baader–Meinhof effect, in which something that has recently come to your attention suddenly seems to appear with improbable frequency shortly afterward—maybe you just bought a red car, and you suddenly start seeing red cars everywhere. The things we spend our time thinking about are the things we tend to notice. It's a wonderful compounding loop: the more gratitude you express, the more you find to be grateful for.

The more grateful you are, the more wonder and joy fills your life. With wonder comes curiosity, and with joy comes an exponential increase in your quality of life and happiness. Gratitude shifts your entire mindset. It pulls your head out of your rear and gets you looking at the world around you, helping you pivot from an "I" to "we" construct. It also moves your focus from what *isn't* working to what *is* working. Something really interesting that often happens is that different areas of your life begin to bleed together. When you start a gratitude practice, you look at your life and take inventory. Often you will notice patterns that crop up in both your personal life and your work life. You can also identify strategies that are working well in your personal life and apply them in your work life, or vice versa.

When I talk to clients about expressing gratitude, they sometimes say something along the lines of "Does this mean

I have to give everyone a thank-you card about everything?" Of course not! However, it *does* mean saying thank you when you're thinking it. Though challenging yourself to express gratitude can be uncomfortable, it makes you better at communicating, which is a cornerstone for strong, healthy relationships, at work and at home.

KEY TAKEAWAYS

Be intentional with your gratitude practice. The intention is the jet fuel—the "Why bother?" Think about what you want to accomplish, why you want to accomplish it, and how you're going to do it. When you go in with a plan or structure, it's easier to do the actual work and gain momentum.

Examine what comes up in your gratitude practice with curiosity and nonjudgment of self. Judgment of self creates limiting beliefs. Rather than judging self, the goal is to seek to align your self to your soul, as is detailed in the next chapter.

FURTHER READING

- *The Psychology of Gratitude*, edited by Robert A. Emmons and Michael E. McCullough
- Greater Good Science Center at UC Berkeley, www.greatergood.berkeley.edu
- *Awakening Compassion at Work*, by Monica Worline and Jane Dutton

CHAPTER 4

UNITING SELF AND SOUL

The merging of self and soul is largely focused around the evolving tenet of graceful leadership. As a reminder, the evolving leader

- is relentless in the pursuit of understanding and aligning self to purpose;
- is a constant learner who is gentle in all pursuits, enlisting a lens of curiosity with a focus on integration; and
- creates relationships that have balance with giving and receiving and does both themselves.

DEFINITION OF SELF AND SOUL

To explain the alignment of self and soul, I must first define what I mean when I say *self* and *soul*. The distinction can be tricky, because both are part of you and they are often intertwined. I've opted for the terminology *self* and *soul*; another way to think about it is as the little self and the big Self—*self*, with a lowercase *s*, and *Self*, with a capital *S*.

Your little self is your ego, the self you've constructed to get through this thing called life. It is created through your life experiences and your environment. Thus, if you were born in different circumstances—in a different country, at a different time, among different people—your little self would develop differently. It is important to note that your ego is *not* "bad." It guides you in how to interact with yourself, others, and the world. It is your human interface—your programming that allows you to survive in this world. In fact, our egos are a large part of our successes.

Your big Self is your soul, the Self that comes with you into this world. Your soul is your essence, the truest expression of who you are. The soul does not take into account this lifetime's environment. If you could rewind the clock and change a person's environment, their little self would change as well; however, their big Self would not. The big Self is immutable. It is pure, innocent, and agenda-free. Though your soul is unique to you, all souls are the same in that they have a divine purpose.

ALIGNMENT OF SELF AND SOUL IN THE MIDDLE OF A PR DISASTER

Daniel was working as the executive vice president for public relations at a transportation company when disaster struck: a pet died while the company was transporting it. In the aftermath, the organization was faced with a seemingly insurmountable task: "What do we do to clean this up? *Can* we even clean it up?" The company needed to protect themselves while simultaneously showing customers that they cared about people and their pets. Most important of all, they needed to make sure this never happened again.

The situation was a particular challenge for Daniel, as the incident was a PR nightmare, to say the least. News of the incident had gotten out, and the company was facing major backlash from every direction. Daniel rose to the challenge and did a beautiful job of being graceful with each stakeholder in the situation, from the person who had lost their pet, to the legal team representing the company, to the workers' union, to the company's stockholders.

In his internal conversations within the company, Daniel exemplified the transparency and evolving tenets of graceful leadership. He was clear and open in his communication, and he approached the situation with gentle curiosity. He acknowledged the problems that had led to the pet's unfortunate death, and he shared what he did and did *not* know of the situation. Rather than becoming defensive and blaming others, he withheld judgment until things could be properly investigated. Though he couldn't give everyone the answers they wanted right away, he promised to follow up with what he didn't yet know.

Daniel also exemplified the connecting tenet. It would have been easy to fall into an us-vs.-them mentality in this situation. For a less graceful leader, it would have felt like it was the company vs. everyone else—the company vs. the person who lost their pet, the animal advocacy organizations, and the public at large. It also would have been easy for the company to find and sacrifice a scapegoat. Specifically, the company had contracted with a vendor, and after an investigation, it was revealed that this vendor was primarily responsible for the equipment failure that had led to the pet's tragic death. Instead of throwing the vendor out front and saying, "It's their fault, not ours," the organization stood next to the vendor. The organization and vendor took responsibility for the problem together. By adopting a "we're in this together" mentality, the organization was able to maintain its professional relationships and was also better able to solve the problem and ensure it never happened again.

Externally, Daniel showed the same grace. He acknowledged what was true and was also quick to dismantle what wasn't true. He didn't shy away from the difficult conversations. In his external communication, while he had to work through the appropriate legal channels, he still strove to craft the communications in a way that acknowledged the damage, loss, and hurt the affected customer was experiencing while not opening the company up to legal issues by taking the blame where it wasn't warranted.

Daniel kept the focus future-oriented by looking at how the company would change its procedures moving forward and what the company could do for the customer in this particular situation. By empathizing with the customer and approaching the situation from the customer's perspective, the organization came up with some creative, thoughtful solutions. Part of the solution involved writing a check. Additionally, the organization reached out to the pet's breeder and sponsored a litter so that when the customer was ready for a new pet, they could have one from the same breeder. Of course, nothing can replace a lost pet, yet the organization did the best they could in the situation.

Daniel showed remarkable alignment of self and soul throughout this challenge. The part of alignment that he was particularly skilled at was being a constant learner who is gentle in all pursuits, enlisting a lens of curiosity. He didn't jump to conclusions. He remained curious and gentle, withholding judgment and not blaming.

MISALIGNMENT OF SELF AND SOUL: PLAYING THE BLAME GAME WITH LOST BAGGAGE

I've only had my luggage lost by an airline once. I was flying a lot at that time, so I had priority baggage handling. My bag was always one of the first to appear on the conveyor belt, so I realized pretty quickly that it was lost.

When I went to the help desk, the first thing the attendant, Jeremy, said after I explained the situation was "You must not have put your priority tag on."

I was a little taken back by this response. *Of course* I hadn't put the priority tag on. I didn't even have access to that tag. It was something airline employees put on when the bag was checked. The tag was definitely put on correctly. I figured Jeremy must be having a bad day, so I let it slide. So I said, "Suspending your judgment of what I did or didn't do, can you help me find my bag?"

They did eventually find the bag. By that time, I had left the airport and was at a retreat center. They agreed to ship the bag to me. I waited. It did not arrive. So I contacted Jeremy about it, and he said, "Well, Ms. Thompson, not only did you not put your right tag on, but the address you gave us for the retreat center was incorrect."

I'm going to be honest: at this point, I fell out of grace and got a little snippy with him. I said, "Let me re-forward you the email with the address, and you tell me where this went wrong." At that point, he had to admit that I'd given him the right address. So he shifted the blame from me to the shuttle service they contracted with to deliver the bags. There was zero accountability on his part.

Throughout our conversations, he mentioned that this kind of issue happened a lot because he had to use three different systems that didn't communicate with each other. I naturally jumped into consultant mode. "How can I help you solve this issue so it doesn't happen anymore? It's pretty inconvenient for all of us, right? And I'm sure it's expensive." He agreed with me. When I suggested he send the problem up the food chain, though, he deflected. I saw all kinds of opportunity for improvement, yet instead of addressing the underlying recurring problems, he decided the solution was to fire the shuttle service, which is exactly what he did. It was a one-time solution that did nothing to address the bigger issues.

It was clear to me that Jeremy was not aligned in self and soul. He wasn't curious about anything in this situation and, if I had to guess, in many other situations as well. He made (wrong) assumptions more than once because of that lack of curiosity. He was also stuck in an "I"-focused perspective, not a "we." From my perspective, he didn't genuinely care about me or my experience. It felt like he saw me as an inconvenience that he wanted to get rid of as quickly as possible. This same "I" focus was apparent when he threw the shuttle service under the bus. The soul by its very nature is interlaced with absolutely every other thing in the universe. When someone is only concerned for themselves, their self and soul cannot be in alignment. This happens to us all at times. Alignment isn't absolute; it ebbs and flows. The goal isn't perfection; it is the experience of more "we" than "I."

ALIGNMENT, NOT ELIMINATION

Resist the urge to see the self and the soul as a dichotomy, as a battle between your ego and your deeper nature. The soul is not "good," and the self is not "bad"; they simply are. The goal is not to eliminate the ego; rather, it is to ensure that your self and soul are aligned.

Oftentimes, we experience a division between who we are at our core and that which we've become based upon our environment. This fracture, or misalignment, can be conscious. Most of the time, though, it's unconscious. The soul does not disappear, yet it becomes laden with our ego. We are all souls having human experiences. Sometimes those human experiences are layered on top of our souls such that our fundamental essence becomes obscured.

The division between self and soul is often subconsciously programmed early in life. When I was young, I played sports. I naturally have a competitive nature, and my experience as an athlete reinforced my innate desire to win. When I performed well as an athlete, I felt *seen*. Coaches would praise me, teammates would pat me on the back, spectators would cheer. When I didn't perform, I felt invisible. My performance and my sense of self-worth subsequently became entwined.

There was one soccer game I remember in which I inadvertently kicked the ball into an opponent's head. I was a powerful kicker, and I knew the blow must have hurt. What I really wanted to do in that situation was call a timeout and make sure my opponent was okay. I didn't feel as if I could do that, though. The ball was still in play, and I had to get it to the end of the field. We ended up scoring, and thus I was rewarded for my lack of compassion. Over time, I stopped caring when I saw players get hurt, because I was seen and valued for *not* caring. This same attitude carried over into my career in corporate America. I only felt seen when I performed, so I did whatever it took to get the results and be seen. The learned behavior of my self overshadowed my soul's instinctive compassion.

People can spend years, decades, or even their whole lives oblivious to the division between their self and soul. Then one day, something happens that triggers a moment of inquiry. It could be a tragedy or a joy or a small, seemingly inconsequential experience. Whatever the case, it is something that pauses them long enough to ask, "Is this it? Is who I think I am the person I actually am?" I work with many people in their forties, fifties, and sixties, and these are exactly the kinds of questions they're wrestling with. They are accomplished professionally, yet something is still missing.

Simply asking these questions is a critical step in your journey into graceful leadership. A graceful leader is curious. He or she asks new, different questions—deep, layered questions that are bigger than the little self. Once you start asking these questions, you are exploring your soul, even if you don't realize it yet. When you ask, "Is who I think I am the person I actually am?" you are acknowledging that there are various expressions of you. While there is only one you, one soul, there are different ways you *act*, based on your ego. When you ask, "Is this it?" you begin thinking about purpose and mission and joy. That is your soul getting your self's attention.

We are both little self and big Self—ego and soul—at any point in time. Remember: the goal is *not* to erase your ego. Your ego serves great purpose. Though it might be ill directed at times or operating from limiting beliefs that you need to upgrade, there's no reason to eradicate it. Your ego is what allows you to navigate this world effectively. So rather than trying to get rid of it, the goal is to find your own personal grace experience. To this end, it is important to develop the ability to be still, evaluate your behaviors, assess how they are working for you, and redeploy differently if needed.

Just as you express curiosity about the outward world, you can do it inwardly as well. Explore inwardly with tenderness, compassion, and self-love. Seek to become observant and aware in the moment. Watch and listen to yourself.

There are times when I will speak not very nicely to someone I love dearly, and in that moment, I will watch and listen to myself. I become awake to what I am doing. With this awareness, I can choose to stop speaking this way. Sometimes I decide that my current behavior is not in alignment with my soul, and I stop. Other times, I decide that my ego-driven behavior is in fact needed for the situation. A good example was the linen-closet crackdown when my kids were in middle school.

My kids did their own laundry starting from a young age because I hated doing it. One day, I thought I'd be nice and put their laundry away for them. I opened up their linen closet to put their towels away and just stood there a moment. You know in cartoons when a character needs to clean quickly, so they throw everything into the closet and then squeeze the door shut to keep it all inside? That was what it looked like. Things were balled up and crammed into every available crevice in the most cluttered, chaotic puzzle I've ever seen.

I calmly knocked on their bedroom doors, and when they came out into the hall, I returned to the closet. And I started pulling every last thing out. Sheets were flying over my head; washcloths were hitting the ceiling. It was a linen whirlwind. Halfway through this, I had this moment of observation where I thought, *Oh my God, you're acting like a crazy woman.* Then I thought, *Hmm, I think they need to see crazy right now.* I wanted to teach them that doing sloppy, careless work isn't a great character trait, and they needed a big reaction from me to learn the lesson. While I was definitely acting from my self and not my soul in that moment, it was what the situation needed. It serves as a great family story now.

THE IMPACTS OF OVERTIME: A GRACEFUL LEADER'S EXPERIENCE ALIGNING SELF AND SOUL

Jackson worked in a manufacturing environment, and there was a big order they needed to get out for a client. Unfortunately, there was an issue in their supply chain, and they were missing a particular part they needed to complete the order. They were waiting and waiting for the part, getting more stressed as the client deadline approached.

Finally, the part arrived, just three weeks before the order was due. To get everything done, they had to work around the clock, three shifts a day, with most employees pulling two shifts almost every day. For nearly an entire month, everyone was working twelve to eighteen hours a day, getting a day off if they could, and then coming back and doing it all over. They ended up meeting and even exceeding the goal a little bit. So from an outside perspective, it worked.

Even though this around-the-clock crunch had worked, Jackson questioned whether it had been worth it. The supply-chain delay was not a one-off issue, which meant this same situation would happen *again and again*. The past month had been hell for Jackson, and he knew it had to have been hell for everybody else too.

At this period in time, Jackson knew he needed to work on empathy. That was part of the reason I was working with him. So he went around and interviewed everyone about the impact the past three weeks had had on their lives. At first, everyone gave him the nice answer: "Oh, everything's okay." Jackson knew that wasn't true. The past month had been objectively hellish; he just wanted to know *how* hellish. He leaned into these conversations and created the space for people to open up. In doing this, he discovered that a lot of people had incurred extra expenses as a result of all the overtime: day care, takeout dinners, even a nonrefundable vacation one employee had to miss. It was sobering to see the emotional, physical, and mental toll the last weeks had taken on people's lives as well as the *financial* toll.

Obviously, this was not a sustainable practice. It simply wasn't worth it. So Jackson went to work to fix the supply-chain issue. Even after refining that process, they were still running into periodic crunch times, though nothing nearly as intense. For those special situations, Jackson helped create a new intentional process that would reduce the number of quality-assurance steps needed, to help ease the burden. One of the most surprising things, was his invitation for everyone to bring in the outside bills they'd incurred, including that missed vacation, and the company paid them back.

Talk about alignment of self and soul! The company wasn't required to pay the employees' personal expenses. However, to be in line with his integrity and vision, Jackson felt like they couldn't *not* do it. As laid out in the evolving tenet, he was showing a balance of giving and receiving in his relationships. His employees had just given him three weeks of their sweat and tears; he wanted to give something back to them. He'd also engaged his curiosity. He looked for and found innovative solutions to their problems and worked very hard to make himself aware of his employees' emotional landscapes. Since self is primarily self-serving, while soul is universe-serving, becoming aware of someone else's emotional landscape brings you outside of little self and into soul. Finally, he was relentless in pursuing his purpose, which was to be a bridge builder, bringing people together. By having those open conversations, he was able to create multiple bridges for people, financially, emotionally, and in terms of performance and relationships.

TAKE A MISALIGNMENT INVENTORY

As you begin to step into your grace center, consider taking an alignment inventory, cataloguing all the times you acted in a way that put your self and soul into misalignment. Though the exercise can be painful, it is also revealing and constructive, giving you the opportunity to release any guilt and shame you may still be holding on to, whether consciously or subconsciously.

Early in my own path to grace, I cataloged *all* the times when I had not been true to my word, where relationships had ended, where relationships were struggling, where I had acted in a way that did not honor my soul—literally every single misalignment. It was jaw-dropping to see the culmination of times when I had not lived into the best version of myself, and the exercise brought up guilt and shame. I beat back the judgment I offered myself and that I received from many of the amazing people I had hurt with my misalignment. It wasn't easy. It was like I was in an echo chamber of negativity: *You're not good enough. You're a fake. You lied. You don't belong.*

Patterns emerged for me to explore, and once I was able to see a few keys ones, it was much easier for me to chart a course and reach out to seek amends where possible. Not everyone was open to receiving this vulnerable version of me. Though it was hard when that happened, letting others be where they chose to be was a humbling part of the process.

One of the most embarrassing misalignments I remembered was a decent-size debt I owed a gentleman for doing some work on a home I lived in for a short time. He had agreed to finish the work based on my word that I would make good on the debt. I had every intention of keeping my word. Then, in the following three weeks, my world unraveled. I moved out of the house and was in the fight of my life for my children. The commitment I had made got lost for a bit. Then the calls started coming for payment. I dodged them for a while and finally took the call one day, dreading the conversation. I did not have the means to keep my word. I explained the situation, and while he said he understood, we could both feel the disappointment and frustration on both sides. I felt like such a schmuck on every level. I promised I would pay him once I was back on my feet.

Fast-forward fifteen years—yes, fifteen years. The debt I owed was this shadow in the back of my mind, feeding the shame and guilt that I was not who I said I was. Once I remembered this debt, I frantically went to the attic and searched through old boxes until I found his name and contact information.

It took me a couple of days to gather the courage to make the call. He certainly remembered who I was. I explained that I was calling to settle the debt. The silence from the other side was thick enough to cut through. He responded that he'd never expected this call, and now that it was here, he was glad it had come.

I sent him a check for the original debt, including a large penalty fee. After putting that check in the mail, I skipped back from the mailbox. The relief that I had realigned my behavior, no matter how old, to the person I said I was evoked great joy.

A couple of weeks later, I received a note from him saying the following: "Not many people would have bothered to 'true up' with this many years gone by. I am so thankful you did; it has restored my faith in people. The money came at a time when we really needed it and never saw it coming. I wish you all the best life has to offer."

Upholding my word and realigning my self and soul was so healing for us both. He extended grace to me, and in turn I was able to offer it to myself. So I encourage you to take inventory of your own misalignments and seek to make amends, no matter how old the transgression may be. Though you can't change the past, you can choose to extend grace in the present, healing old wounds and building alignment for the future.

BEARING WITNESS TO THE ALIGNING OF SELF AND SOUL

To bear witness to your aligning of self and soul, seek to spend time in between the two. This means recognizing that *you are not your ego*. You do this by first becoming aware of your ego. You're not making it wrong or trying to shed it like a snakeskin; you're owning it—all of it, the glory of it and the yuckiness of it. At the same time, you're learning to observe your ego as a part of you and not your whole being. As humans, we have multiple dimensions; the ego is just one. When you become the observer, you are bearing witness.

> *By practising introspection or focused "I" gazing, moments of grace may occur in which the moving waters of your interior become still.*
>
> —KEN WILBER, *INTEGRAL LIFE PRACTICE*

As you bear witness, you can begin to adjust your behavior to bring your self more in alignment with your soul. One great way to do this is to express your power while holding your compassion. Our souls are innately compassionate, so when you seek to act with compassion, your self will more closely align with your soul. For instance, if someone is screaming at you, you can say, "I hear you. However, I'm unwilling to have this conversation while you're yelling." You can set these boundaries while remaining compassionate, and in this way, you increase your alignment.

Another way to increase your alignment is to identify times you were not aligned and try to fix them. We often think that once something is done, it's done, and there's no going back. That is not true. Although you might not be able to go back and *erase* a mistake or start over with a completely clean slate, you *can* go back and acknowledge that you made a mistake. If you're willing to be courageous and eat some humble pie, then more often than not, you can clean up and correct your past mistakes. Acknowledging bad decisions also allows us to do things in a different, more-aligned way in the future.

We all exhibit a spectrum of behaviors. Sometimes we're quiet; other times we're loud and boisterous. Pay attention to the full range of your behavior. Notice when you're extending yourself to others more and when you're becoming more hermitlike. Become aware of your different ways of being and doing in the world. You can have an alignment of self and soul in a wide variety of ways. Whether you're joyous or sad or angry or peaceful, you can still be in alignment. Martin Luther King Jr., for instance, understood that righteous anger was a powerful tool to be utilized in pursuing and aligning to purpose. Being in alignment does not mean you must always be calm and peaceful, though that is one way of being in alignment. Shifting into the awareness of alignment and misalignment is a gritty process. It asks of us great resolve and stillness as we do this inner mining. This process will bring into awareness limiting beliefs. It can be startling—remember to be kind and graceful with yourself as you unwind some of your unconscious behaviors.

As I mentioned previously, the soul is naturally connected to the wider world. So for more alignment, moving from an "I" perspective to a "we" perspective is critical. Note that moving to a "we" perspective does not mean that you lose the "I" perspective. You can hold both at the same time. You can have a "we" perspective while retaining your personal authenticity and uniqueness. The issue is simply that many of us are weighted too heavily toward the "I" perspective and need to achieve more balance.

> *Letting go of our egocentric selves by serving others is the first step to finding our true selves. In caring for other human beings we discover ourselves and a joy that we cannot acquire when we are focused on self-promotion and self-protection.*
> —A. G. LAFLEY AND ROGER L. MARTIN, *PLAYING TO WIN*

A final strategy to help you better align is to move toward relationships you would have previously avoided, assuming they are safe. Oftentimes certain relationships with people look too intimidating, difficult, scary, or inconvenient to pursue. It is your ego giving you those messages, and since the ego often carries baggage, those messages may no longer be relevant. It's worth analyzing those judgments. It's like a dog I once knew who was afraid of men with beards who wore baseball hats because of a negative experience early in life. Are all men with beards and baseball hats actually bad? Of course not. Some of them give great neck scratches. We must closely examine the information our egos have been imprinted with. Otherwise, we could be missing out on rewarding relationships.

Along the same lines, it is important to examine your current relationships to determine whether they are serving you. As you align more with your soul, you will likely discover things that you are no longer willing to tolerate.

KEY TAKEAWAYS

Your self and soul are at play all the time, and they're both doing exactly what they need to do. Neither one is wrong or better than the other. Your role is to observe what they are doing so that you can choose which strategies and ways of being are needed for a particular situation.

There are graceful and graceless leaders in our world, and the same individual can be graceful in one moment and graceless in the next. Start to develop an awareness of these characteristics in your own life, both in your own leadership and in leaders around you.

Work toward a perspective of nonduality. Seemingly contradictory things can exist simultaneously. Acknowledging that multiple perspectives can be equally true leads to less judgment, which is a key part of distinguishing story from fact, as we will explore in the next chapter.

FURTHER READING

- *Playing to Win*, by A. G. Lafley and Roger L. Martin
- *Integral Life Practice*, by Ken Wilber, Terry Patten, Adam Leonard, and Marco Morelli
- *Mastering Leadership*, by Robert J. Anderson and William A. Adams

CHAPTER 5

USE GRACE TO DISTINGUISH STORY FROM FACT

Rushing to judgment is a common sabotaging habit of all humans, not just leaders. Judgment is a self-protective instinct. We tend to move forward in situations as though our perception is truth. The person on the other side of the conflict does the same thing. When our two "truths" clash, we butt heads and start pointing fingers. To break out of this never-ending finger-pointing game, we must learn to distinguish perception from truth, story from fact.

FIXING A "SHITSTORM": MOVING BEYOND STORY TO THE FACTS

José was a senior vice president for a manufacturing company. I'd been working with the organization for a few years deploying StrengthsFinder and teamwork exercises, and one day José called me and said, "Lexy, I need you to get in here and help me figure this situation out before I cut everyone off at the knees." I could hear in his voice that he was stressed out. "This is a shitstorm," he told me. While it wasn't the most eloquent way of putting it, as he explained the situation to me, I understood why he felt that way.

José was in charge of several different manufacturing facilities. He traveled a lot between locations, and it was on a routine visit to one of his facilities that he unearthed the "shitstorm." Orders were getting messed up, and it was one problem after another after another. Three major problems stood out: they were consistently off on measurements while milling parts; they were shipping the wrong parts to clients; and they were botching handoffs between different manufacturing processes.

At this time, the organization was looking at acquiring other companies as well as potentially being acquired themselves. There were already a lot of moving parts, and the last thing José wanted was more problems at an already high-stress time. It was the perfect storm. José was especially frustrated because he felt blindsided by these problems. He is a methodical, reliable, analytical guy, and he'd done a good job of surrounding himself with talented people. Everything had been working smoothly for the previous two years—no mismeasurements, no silly shipping errors, no quality issues.

There hadn't been any large changes that José could see, yet now, all of a sudden, it seemed as if nothing was working like it should. With his frustration, stress, and concern building, José desperately wanted to understand what was happening. So he created a story to make sense of the situation. The story he told himself was that his team of leaders below him were incompetent. It was their job to keep this facility running smoothly, and they were failing to do that. The other facilities weren't having these problems, so it had to be an issue with these leaders.

Although this was only a story, not the facts, we tend to move forward as though our perception is truth. So José called a war-room meeting, and he let his team have it. He wasn't verbally abusive or inappropriate. He is typically mild-mannered, though, so anytime he raises his voice, people sit up straight and pay attention. He essentially told them, "This is unacceptable. This isn't working, and something needs to change."

Though José was skilled in giving feedback in a constructive, even graceful way, he wasn't being a graceful leader in this situation. A graceful leader operates from a place of curiosity. If you get stuck in a story, accepting your judgments as fact, you lose curiosity. José's story was that his leaders were incompetent. The moment he accepted that narrative as fact instead of story, he stopped looking for other explanations. That hindered his ability to properly address the problems, because, as we would soon discover, he hadn't found the true cause of the issues.

Even as José was running the story that his team was incompetent, part of him knew that it wasn't true. The leaders below him were mostly the same people doing the same thing they'd been doing for years. It didn't make sense that they were competent last year and suddenly incompetent this year. That was part of the reason he called me. He knew he was missing *something*.

When I came in, the first thing I had José do was suspend everything—all judgments. Maybe his team *was* incompetent. We couldn't know that yet, though, not until we investigated further. So he and I got into a room, and for almost two hours we did a SWOT (strengths, weaknesses, opportunities, and threats) analysis to figure out exactly what had changed. We engaged our curiosity and moved past the initial story that the leadership team was the issue.

We started asking questions. Since the internal team has been pretty static, what was happening externally? Were we getting good materials in? Were we getting good direction from our clients? We brainstormed all the possibilities we could imagine. We ended up finding some interesting things.

First, we figured out a way to improve communication between two different shipping vendors to prevent so many shipping mistakes. Then we discovered that there was a client error related to the schematics. A vendor was working from one set of directions, and the in-house staff of the manufacturing facility were working from a different set. The two sets of instructions were supposed to line up, and they didn't. The error was corrected, and the loss of material from mismeasurements was absorbed by the client, because it was their error. So it wasn't that José's staff was stupid and unable to measure parts, as he'd originally assumed. In the grand scheme of things, both of these issues were relatively small, easy fixes, yet if José hadn't suspended his judgment, these solutions wouldn't have been discovered and implemented nearly as quickly, leading to lost revenue for the company.

The other problem we discovered was a little more complicated. Somewhat recently, José had been put in charge of two more regions. With the extra responsibilities, he needed to streamline the chain of command and increase the efficiency of communication. This meant reducing the number of people he had to interact with. To do this, he promoted one of his direct reports over another one of his direct reports. It made sense in theory. What inadvertently happened, though, was the start of a turf war.

The two direct reports, Anika and George, were initially great friends who worked well together. Then all of a sudden, Anika was George's boss. José did not do a good job of communicating his intention with this change. One day, George was his own boss, reporting directly to José, and then the next day, he was reporting to Anika, with no understanding of why. George and Anika began to butt heads. They started to triangulate their teams below them instead of working together as they had before.

This is another place where José could have easily fallen into story and chosen to blame George and Anika for their infighting. Instead, he kept himself open to their perspective and owned the fact that he had created confusion for them. He called them into his office to apologize and explain his intention with the promotion.

Once he'd explained the goal he was working toward—streamlined communication and fewer direct reports—he asked George and Anika for their input. Though he had savvy leaders below him, he wasn't treating them that way. Instead of bringing them into the problem-solving process, he'd simply assumed that his solution—promoting Anika—was the right one. Now he opened himself to the possibility that maybe there was a different, better solution out there.

It's a good thing he did, because Anika and George delivered. They came back to him with the recommendation that instead of promoting Anika, he promote Darryl, whom they both respected. Darryl had been overlooked because he was a quiet guy. He was really, really good at his job, though, and he ended up being the perfect fit. It was a win for everyone involved. José reduced his direct reports, Darryl got a promotion, the manufacturing facility got the leadership it needed, and Anika and George got a work environment they could thrive in. Before this organizational change, Anika and George had begun considering leaving the company because of their dissonant relationship. Instead, the company was able to retain them as talented leaders, and they both ended up being promoted into other regions within a year.

Most impressive, this complete turnaround of the manufacturing facility took *less than a month*! If José had remained stuck in his story, it would have taken far longer to correct these issues. The company almost certainly would have lost clients and money in the process too.

CURIOSITY—ELIMINATOR OF JUDGMENT

As humans, we love patterns. So much of our lives is dictated by patterns and habits. It makes us efficient, sometimes at the expense of effectiveness. Sometimes the patterns we're operating from are based on inaccurate or incomplete information. Curiosity is our tool for pattern interruption.

Curiosity and judgment cannot coexist. As soon as you stop

and ask a question, you create space between your thought and the inquiry. In that space, you have a choice. You may end up choosing to judge. Until you make that choice, though, the judgment does not exist. You can't be judging while you're still choosing. If you slow everything down to ask, "Why would a good and decent person do that?" or "How did this come to happen?" or whatever the inquiry might be, it allows you to step outside of your story and consider other potential answers. That is curiosity doing its job.

Graceful leaders are not married to their story. By being open to other facts beyond their own perspective, graceful leaders can make more-informed decisions that consider the big picture of a situation. For this reason, they tend to make decisions that are for the greater good, not just for the specific moment in time or for the specific individual in front of them. They don't feel a need to be right, and they are curious about others' perspectives, like José recognizing that Anika and George might have a better solution than his. Graceful leaders want the *best* solution, not *their* solution. It takes confident, self-assured leaders to empower their staff to make intelligent, competent decisions without being micromanaged. Although leaders always say they would love to have a team like that, it can be unnerving to have a high-performing team that seemingly doesn't need you. The idea that empowering your team diminishes your own power is simply another story we tell ourselves, though. An empowered team is a sign of a powerful leader.

THE PITFALLS OF JUDGMENT

It was winter in Vermont, and I was working at the car dealership as a salesperson. You don't sell a lot of cars in winter. If someone comes looking for a car in the winter, though, they're usually serious. We worked totally on commission, so things could be a little cutthroat. However, we did have a system where we took turns with customers whenever someone came onto the lot.

On this particular day, a young woman arrived on the lot decked out in ski gear. The guy whose turn it was took one look at her and said, "You can have her." I wasn't about to turn down a potential sale, even if it might look like the customer wasn't serious.

Well, turns out that young woman was Diann Roffe, a US Olympic skier. Even better, she already knew exactly what she wanted. She essentially just handed me a check and said, "Put the order through." It was one of the easiest sales of my life. And that's a firsthand example of why you don't judge a book by its cover.

Judgments of any kind can cause missed opportunities and mischief. It's easy to see how judgments of something as bad can be a problem. However, even judgments of something as *good* is an issue. For instance, I once worked with a woman with incredibly strong relational skills, Jan. One of Jan's direct reports came to her and told her that a fellow employee, Pete, was going through a divorce and struggling. Jan thought this was great, because she was now in a place to be more helpful and empathetic to Pete. Jan lightened Pete's workload so he could start getting out right at five and could pick his son up from day care. This might seem like the kind, graceful thing to do. From Pete's perspective, though, Jan was taking away his responsibilities, and he didn't know why. He started to worry that he wasn't doing a good job. Jan, with the best of intentions, had actually made his situation harder and more stressful.

When the employee first came to tell her about Pete, Jan's judgment was that receiving this information was a good thing. If she had questioned that judgment, she may have considered that it was wrong to receive this kind of personal information from someone other than Pete. Maybe she then would have chosen to stop the conversation and establish boundaries when it comes to sharing personal information in the workplace.

There's often not a right or wrong answer in a given situation. The important thing is to consider all of the answers so that you can make the best decision you can. Question *all* your judgments, good and bad.

DISTINGUISHING STORY FROM FACT

The first step to distinguishing story from fact is asking

open-ended, powerful questions. These questions tend to focus on *why* and *how*. Here are a few of my favorite questions that are applicable to many situations:

- Why would someone I like behave this way?
- What could be impacting this person to cause them to behave this way?
- If it were me, how would I handle this situation?

You can easily adapt these questions to start conversations with others:

- Can you help me understand how you got here?
- What has changed to create these new behaviors?
- How would you solve this issue?

In asking these questions, it is important to understand that you can have a fact, and someone else can have a fact, and even if those two facts look in opposition to each other, they can both be true. As a simple example, a dog can be cute and terrifying at the same time. A person with a fear of dogs who has been bitten before will find the dog scary. That is a fact. On the other hand, someone who has only had good experiences with dogs will only think of the dog as cute. That is also fact. Both of those perspectives are valid and true for the people experiencing them. Now, if we were to say the dog is *vicious*, we would be slipping into story territory, as the dog may or may not be vicious.

Hold the awareness that every perspective is both true and partial, including your own. Thus, try to be less defensive of your point of view and more curious about and open to new ways of seeing things.

—KEN WILBER, *INTEGRAL LIFE PRACTICE*

When you feel annoyed, criticized, or superior, check in on your judgments. Whether your initial reaction is "Oh my God, this is terrible" or "Oh, lovely, that's wonderful," take a moment to question the judgments of the situation. When we are feeling defensive, it's hard to hear other possibilities. We feel as if we are under attack, so old reptilian patterns click on in the back of our brain, triggering fight-or-flight mechanisms of protection. In these situations, we frequently dig our heels in and cling to our story. We must make a conscious effort to pull ourselves out of that instinctual, knee-jerk reaction. Similarly, when we're getting praise and it's everything we want to hear, we construct a story of cotton-candy perfection. That is no more true than a story of doom and gloom. Becoming aware of these judgments and recognizing that they are not fact is incredibly helpful.

For example, say an assistant tells the CEO that they are running late. The CEO feels annoyed and rushed and thinks the assistant is being overly critical. Her first impulse is to tell the assistant he needs to be more flexible. Then she pauses and asks herself, "Why is my assistant telling me this?" After some thought, she realizes that the assistant isn't trying to be annoying or critical; rather, when she's running late, it hinders his ability to do his job. At that point, they can talk about the issue and generate solutions, like creating more buffers in the CEO's calendar.

Distinguishing story from fact requires that you inquire about others' experiences. We're not mind readers; if we want to know about somebody else's perspective, the easiest thing to do is *ask*. Jackson, from the story in chapter 4, where his employees worked around the clock for nearly a month, is a good example of the power of inquiry. By asking his employees about the impacts of such a strenuous work schedule, he was able to uncover the hidden truths of the situation.

THE DANGER OF STAYING IN STORY

Mara worked in a hospital system department that had long functioned from a command-and-control model of leadership. While a graceful leader doesn't require formal authority to lead, command-and-control leaders rely on it. Whenever Mara was questioned or challenged, she would say, "Because I'm your boss" or "Because I said so."

This approach did *not* go over well with her subordinates. Though she wasn't aware of it, she was slowly creating layers of alienation between her and her team. Her team was also learning to only do things when they were told to do them.

That meant no ingenuity, no collaboration, no innovative problem-solving.

The hospital system had long wanted to shift their leadership paradigm to be more collaborative, and they decided they were serious about it this time. Mara, though, did not take it seriously. She was stuck in her story. She had always led from authority, and she couldn't tap into curiosity to consider why that might not be the best way to lead people. She refused to alter her behavior and leadership style. Because she would not get on board with the hospital system's desired changes, they fired her.

Even if it doesn't cause you to lose your job like Mara, staying in story can still have dangerous consequences. Among the most critical is that you stop growing. When you accept your story as fact, you develop a belief that you know it all. That is the deadliest story of all. You stop looking for new information, and you cut off anything that might challenge your assumptions. As a result, you stop learning, and you eliminate opportunities for connection. You miss out on the possibility of exploring other solutions and ways of being.

You don't lose anything by being open to new information. Either you change your original position because you are now more informed, which is great, or you confirm your original position, which is also great.

As a somewhat trivial example, I hated Texas in the summer because it got unbearably hot. In my mind, it was just utterly miserable. It became a self-fulfilling prophecy for me. I thought summers in Texas were hot and miserable, so guess what: I felt hot and miserable. Then one day while I was at a restaurant, I was chatting with a woman who told me, "I love this hot weather!" My first thought was, *What is wrong with you?* As she explained, I started to understand. She loved spending the summers in her pool with her grandkids, and she loved how refreshing a blast of air-conditioning was after soaking in the sun. Those were things she couldn't experience in the winter months.

I still don't love the heat. After that conversation, though, I shifted my mindset. Instead of sticking to my story that summer was miserable and hot, I focused on the things I *did* like about the summer, like homemade, fresh-squeezed organic lemonade. June, July, and August became my lemonade months instead of my months of hell. I also loved to take cold outdoor showers in the summer and made an effort to incorporate those into my routine. While there were still days when I was hot and miserable, they were not nearly as frequent as before. If I'd stayed in story, I would've only been hurting myself by being more miserable than I needed to be.

With grace, perfection isn't the goal. Being a graceful leader is being the leader that is needed in the moment, not being a "perfect" leader. Perfection, as most people define it, is the annihilation of almost everything good; it's a joy killer. It's a pursuit for an imagined state of being that rarely exists and is never sustainable. Perfection is the grandest illusion. When people talk about "perfection," they're actually talking about a story they have of the way things "should" be. Everything is already completely perfect, just the way it is. Our idea of perfection is a constant future state that is "better" than whatever we have or are right now. True perfection is being present in the moment. There is no past or future for grace, only the present.

We're human beings. We're going to make mistakes. We're going to trip and fall down. We're going to be ungraceful sometimes, and that's okay. As long as you are *aware* of your behavior and not sleeping through it, you are on the right track. There is no perfect being of grace to attain. If you hold on to the story of perfection when it comes to grace, you will actually become less graceful instead of more graceful.

THE ADVANTAGE OF GRACE

Grace has the ability to change individuals, teams, organizations, and the world. Part of the power of grace is that it has no agenda. It trusts that what's supposed to happen is going to happen. This doesn't mean it's lazy or not committed. The graceful leader uses discernment, sets boundaries, and strives toward the tenets of grace. Ultimately, though, grace surrenders to what is. This is a huge advantage, because there is no person on earth who is more powerful than someone who has nothing to lose. The graceful leader doesn't hold on to story, so they don't have story to lose. They are not attached to the outcome.

As an example, years ago, I sometimes got into bidding wars for consulting contracts. I had maybe just a dozen employees at the time, and we were often up against much bigger fish in the pond. Each time, I would play to win, and then I let go. I trusted that if the contract was for us, we would get it, and if it wasn't for us, we wouldn't. Whatever the outcome, it would be the best thing for us. When you adopt this perspective, competition becomes obsolete; if the outcome of the competition doesn't matter to you, you can't get caught in damaging competitiveness. Sometimes we won the contracts, and sometimes we didn't. In all instances, the letting go was key. If I didn't let go, I would have overcommitted our resources and lowballed our services. I would have been less effective and more stressed. By letting go, I didn't get stuck pining over what-ifs, and when we did win the contracts, we established a relationship as an equal, collaborative partner as opposed to being a servant to the client.

If we are listening deeply, we'll also feel when it is time to let go, when it is time to let grace do what only grace can do. We'll know when it's time to open and let go of any amount of striving or struggling, which

may include letting go of inquiry or questioning.
There's a time to know when you've done everything
there is for you to do, when you've accomplished your
goal, and when you need to let go and let something
other than your illusionary sense of self take over.
—ADYASHANTI, *THE END OF YOUR WORLD*

Graceful leaders are more adaptable. Adaptability is a huge advantage because the world of work is constantly, rapidly changing. In the current world of business, there is a lot of management that goes around change. Companies design whole new processes in order to make changes; when they identify something that isn't working, they tear it down and completely rebuild it. In *Reinventing Organizations*, Laloux argues that this rigidity of change management will become no longer relevant as new business structures develop. With graceful leadership, business structures are more fluid. Instead of tearing down and rebuilding, the graceful leader pivots and adapts.

Laloux compares human beings to "strings, capable of playing many different notes. The range of the notes they can play depends on the range of tensions they have learned to accommodate."[5] The graceful leader can play many different notes. They don't need to throw the instrument out and get a new one; they simply adjust the tension.

---

5   Laloux, *Reinventing Organizations*, 39.

We're moving away from industrial management. Command-and-control strategies made sense in the industrial age because they created safety and order for large groups of people doing repetitive work. Today, consciousness and technology are changing the structure and philosophy of the workplace. The repetitive work of the industrial age is disappearing as more and more of these tasks are automated, and younger generations respond to different types of leadership because of their higher levels of consciousness.

Though the new work environment is different, many organizations have yet to shift their management style accordingly. In the same way that we, as individuals, must shed limiting beliefs if they are no longer serving us, our organizations must shed old structures. To be most effective in today's workplace, leadership must become more collaborative and interconnected. Grace creates room for everybody to step into their power. Everyone has everyone else's back, so no one has to watch their own back. That opens up so much extra time and energy for innovation and collaboration. Graceful leadership allows employees, teams, groups, and organizations to function better and so allows companies to better serve their clients, their communities, and our world.

KEY TAKEAWAYS

Think about how you are doing the story vs. fact dance in your life. What stories are you telling yourself? Are there assumptions or attachments to outcome that you need to let go of?

Letting go of story allows for my truth and your truth to coexist. This allows for deeper, more effective communication, which means greater resilience and capability to navigate alternative solutions when conflict arises, ultimately leading to better conflict management. In the next chapter, we will look at the role grace plays in conflict.

FURTHER READING

- *The End of Your World*, by Adyashanti
- *Reinventing Organizations*, by Frederic Laloux
- *Difficult Conversations*, by Douglas Stone, Bruce Patton, and Sheila Heen

CHAPTER 6

GRACE IN THE FACE OF CONFLICT

Grace is a wonderful asset in navigating conflict. It prevents us from rushing to judgment and encourages us to consider situations from others' point of view. Grace leads to conversations instead of arguments.

GRACE THROUGH CONFLICT: A SOLUTION TO AN APPARENT CATCH-22

A 3-D printing company was struggling with unsold inventory. It was unrecognized revenue sitting on the shelf, costing the company storage fees. Elizabeth, the VP of marketing, was told to get it off the shelves. These were big-ticket items, and normally, she would produce flyers and attend conferences to sell them. To do that, she needed a budget of close to $200,000. However, Simon, the CFO, would not release any capital to help her market the products, because it wasn't in the budget. They entered into a kind of stalemate. Elizabeth needed money to unload the inventory, and Simon didn't have any money to give her. So the inventory continued to sit on the shelf.

After a while, the CEO got involved and told Elizabeth, "We're not seeing the sales expected. We need to fix this." Elizabeth didn't want to throw Simon under the bus, yet she needed a solution if she was going to satisfy the CEO. She was stuck between a rock and a hard place with an impossible task: moving a significant chunk of inventory with zero budget.

After Elizabeth had beaten around the bush a little bit, the CEO realized that the lack of resources was the issue. So he went and talked to Simon, who explained with transparency that there were no funds in the marketing budget. Like Elizabeth, Simon wanted to be graceful. Though he couldn't currently give Elizabeth any money, he suggested that the CEO could transfer funds from a different budget. He explained the risks involved in that and how long it would take to replenish that other budget. The CEO agreed with Simon's recommendation. Elizabeth got the money she needed, and her team was able to clear out the backlog of the inventory.

In conflict, we tend to tell ourselves stories. In this example, Elizabeth, Simon, and the CEO could have easily fallen into damaging stories that increased the conflict. Elizabeth could have thought, *Great, one more time they're not giving me resources and overpromising my services. I want to do the work but can't.* Simon could have thought, *Great, the company invested in this inventory because sales said they could sell it. They didn't do their job, so now I'm the bad guy because I can't give marketing the money they need. My hands are tied here.* And the CEO could have thought, *I can't trust my team. Why didn't they figure this out beforehand? Why do they need me to handhold them through this?*

With stories like these, there's a lot of finger pointing and mudslinging. Nobody wants to look bad, so they double down and start acting defensively. At that point, instead of working together to solve the real problem, the three involved parties must instead work through the relational conflicts that have been created.

Both Elizabeth and Simon deployed more grace and gave each other the benefit of doubt. They understood that they were both in a tricky situation, so they didn't make the CEO take sides. The CEO also showed them both great empathy. He didn't criticize them for needing help navigating the conflict and readily lent his support as facilitator. With transparency, they were all able to acknowledge each other's challenges and collaborate to find a suitable solution. If Elizabeth had come in blaming Simon, he would have been much less willing to search for a solution like he did. However, because Elizabeth acknowledged his difficulties, Simon was more inclined to help. Instead of fighting each other, they were fighting the issue at hand.

CREATING ROOM FOR GRACE IN CONFLICT

When you create room for grace in conflict, it is no longer about winning and losing. Everybody gets to show up and be the greatest version of themselves. They don't need to get defensive and devolve into lesser behaviors. Instead of us-vs.-them dichotomies, they recognize that a problem exists—such as there's no money in the budget—and it's no one's fault. It is, however, everyone's responsibility to figure out a solution.

A "WE" space exists when there is mutual recognition, communication, and shared understanding.
—KEN WILBER, *INTEGRAL LIFE PRACTICE*

In a business, you're frequently dealing with resource constraints, whether it's time, money, or people, and trying to satisfy multiple stakeholders. Suspending your own needs enough to be curious helps you to be graceful and figure out what other people's needs are. Grace provides the space for everyone's voices to be heard. The leader can then take all the voices into account in order to make the most suitable decision.

DO YOU OPERATE FROM SELF OR SOUL DURING CONFLICT?

When we face conflict, it's easy to fall into unhealthy patterns in which we operate from our self, or ego. This approach tends to create stronger divides instead of resolutions.

Here are some signs you are operating from your self during conflict:

- You are using more "I" statements to prove a point or win.
- You are speaking over others.
- You are not able to paraphrase back what the other party is saying to you.
- You find it hard to celebrate others' wins.
- Being right is the measure of success.
- You consistently bring the conversation back to you.
- You offer a defensive response to most situations.
- You do not extend yourself to help others.
- You manipulate others and situations to your desires.

When you instead operate from your soul in conflict, you leave room for grace. With grace, you are better positioned to resolve instead of "win" the conflict.

Here are some signs you are operating from your soul during conflict:

- You are present in the conversation, seeing and feeling what the other person is experiencing.
- You lose time in the task.
- You are smiling more than usual.
- You are comfortable being uncomfortable.
- You express and receive gratitude with ease and grace.
- You see opportunities to help and step in to offer what is needed.
- You find that things that used to irritate you, just don't.

Without grace, leaders can easily make decisions that result in fallout later—they might fix one thing only to break another. Even seemingly small decisions can spiral into negative consequences if they are made without considering everyone's voices. A good example of this kind of fallout is when José promoted Anika over George in the manufacturing example from the previous chapter. In trying to solve one problem, he actually created more issues for himself.

If Elizabeth, Simon, and the CEO hadn't extended each other grace, they wouldn't have solved the problem nearly as quickly. The CEO might have simply dictated to the CFO what to do, which may not have been as good of a solution as what the CFO ended up proposing. When people collaborate on a solution, then everyone is on board for implementation. Performance and speed are then increased.

THE GRACEFUL TENETS IN ACTION: ELIZABETH, SIMON, AND CEO

All six tenets of graceful leadership are embodied in this example with Elizabeth, Simon, and the CEO.

Tough conversations can threaten our identity, which makes the integrating tenet of graceful leadership critical. If you don't know your truth, it's easier to accept external truths that are placed on you. That means if you don't have an awareness of who you are—mind, body, and soul—it's easier to fall victim to the stories we tell ourselves. If Elizabeth, Simon, and the CEO weren't integrated as individuals, they would have more easily fallen into roles of victim or villain.

The three of them were transparent as well, especially in their communication. They were honest and clear with their intentions. Transparency also came in the form of recognizing that they were not their labels. For instance, Simon understood he was the CFO and also Simon. His role was CFO, and he brought with him all of himself. Labels are a type of story. Becoming aware that we have a story or label playing out in a situation is the first step. Simon recognized that his role as CFO was to be the bad guy; however, though that might be his role, it wasn't his truth. He rejected the label of "bad guy" and subverted that role by co-creating a solution instead of saying no. When we're able to take ourselves out of our role, we can effect a greater congruence between who we truly are and what we do.

For evolving, they suspended judgment and expressed curiosity. Simon got curious about potential solutions after the CEO intervened, and that made Elizabeth show up in a more collaborative way, leading right into the connecting tenet. Simon, Elizabeth, and the CEO didn't fall into an us-vs.-them dichotomy. They didn't play victim or victor. Each person involved understood that they weren't the only one in the conflict. They were in it together (a "we" mindset). That attitude prompted them to co-create, finding innovative solutions. The way the CFO and VP of marketing worked together was certainly a nontraditional problem-solving method.

Finally, the three were compassionately powerful. They were openhearted and came together in this situation by clarifying the terms, the goals, and the purpose. When we don't judge or finger-point, our hearts stay open. The energy exchange between individuals is much faster when hearts are open. If I have my hand over my heart and your hand is over yours, we will struggle to reach a deeper connection. Even if you are working from an open heart, your energy must still pierce through my hand to get to my heart. That creates friction that can be misunderstood by the receiving part. It's far better if all parties come to the table with open hearts. With these open hearts, Simon, Elizabeth, and the CEO figured out how to help everybody get what they needed for the common good of the organization.

LEANING INTO CONFLICT NAVIGATION

One of my clients came to me one day and said, "Oh my God, you're going to kill me. I was talking to my team, and I got a little heated, and I wasn't very graceful. I feel so awful."

First, I let her know that being ungraceful was not cause for feeling awful. Remember: awareness, not perfection, is the goal. Then I asked her for more information about what had happened.

"Did the situation warrant getting upset?" I asked.

She nodded. "It did."

"Were you disrespectful or unkind with your words or body language?"

"No."

"Then were you really ungraceful?"

"No, I guess I wasn't."

Grace is power, and power holds its place. Accordingly, graceful leaders lean into conflict instead of avoiding it. With stillness, they are able to be inside the conflict. They are not positional or judgmental or poised for flight. They approach the conflict with heart, ears, and mind open. They recognize that people are not their behavior. While that makes them compassionate, it doesn't mean they tolerate bad behavior— the exact opposite. Graceful leaders have clear boundaries and believe in compassionate accountability.

You can hold somebody responsible for their actions while holding compassion for them as a person. We can all change our behavior. If you, as a graceful leader, allow bad behavior to continue, you are doing your followers a disservice. As Brené Brown said, "Clear is kind. Unclear is unkind."[6] It is better to establish and adhere to clear guidelines and consequences for behavior than to be unclear with your message.

When I was very young, in one of my first manager roles at a grocery store, I had to let an employee go for stealing. This was before I'd begun my exploration of grace, and I did not handle the situation with compassionate power. I jumped to judgment, labeling the employee who had stolen as a thief. Later in life, I happened to hear about this employee's daughter, who had gone off to college and accomplished some incredible things. In hearing the daughter's story, I discovered that the employee had stolen from the store in order to feed their family. It was like my entire worldview shifted in that moment, like an anvil had dropped on my head to remind me that people are complex. Someone could steal and be a great parent at the same time.

From that point on, when I had to let people go for egregious acts, like stealing, I never said or insinuated that they were bad people. I still terminated their employment, though, because consequences are consequences. If I were to teach them that stealing would be tolerated, it would lead to more-harmful behavior down the line. At the same time, I understood that someone must be in a really bad place if

6   Brown, *Dare to Lead*, 48.

stealing was a viable option. I extended compassion for that reason. I actually had an employee I fired for stealing tell me, "Thank you for acknowledging that I was in a tough place, and thank you for holding me accountable to the fact that the decision I made wasn't the right decision."

KEY TAKEAWAYS

Grace requires confidence to step into the conflict and not run. When you're operating from a need to "win," you will fall into a me-vs.-them mindset, which compounds the negative impacts of conflict without grace. With grace, you can step outside of this construct and instead choose to co-create a solution that benefits the "we," which includes the "I."

Open, graceful communication produces transparency, trust, and a clear-eyed view of what's possible and what's at risk. Not everyone will always get what they want. With grace, though, they can reach a compromise that takes into account the larger whole.

Grace in conflict allows individuals to show up as the best version of themselves, able to fully contribute their talents. This is better for both the company and for the individuals involved. When even just one person shows up with grace at work, they have the power to shift the company culture, which is the topic of our next chapter.

FURTHER READING

- *Behaving as if the God in All Life Mattered*, by Machaelle Small Wright
- *Power vs. Force*, by David Hawkins
- *Crucial Conversations*, by Kerry Patterson, Joseph Grenny, Ron McMillan, and Al Switzler

CHAPTER 7

HOW GRACE CAN TRANSFORM A COMPANY'S CULTURE

From the moment you get into a leadership position, a worthwhile goal is to create such awareness and competence around you that you could leave and nothing would change. A single graceful leader can have this kind of lasting impact on a company's culture.

THE POWER OF GRACE: COMPLETE TURNAROUND IN A YEAR AND A HALF

Nadia was a finance executive in a global healthcare system.

She was a perfectionist, with a command-and-control leadership style. She'd been called a "battle-ax." She was very linear and had high executing skills, which had allowed her to rise to senior VP, where she was running billions of dollars in business.

Like many leaders, Nadia struggled to shift from executing to influencing. She struggled to delegate. She was often out on the floor, looking in people's queues and completing tasks that were two layers below the level she wanted to be focusing on. When there were problems, she found it easier to fix it herself than to let her team figure it out. If you've ever had a boss like this, you can probably imagine how her frequent hovering and micromanaging grated on her team.

The boiling point came when she was accused of racism. What had happened was her office was relocated approximately thirty miles away, from the city to the suburbs. Though Nadia didn't have anything to do with the decision to relocate, the move happened to bring the office closer to her home. At the same time, the move resulted in a longer, more difficult commute for many of the organization's minority employees who lived in the city. A full investigation concluded that the racism accusations were unfounded. During the investigation, some areas of improvement did present themselves for Nadia, and the organization offered her an executive coach. That is when I entered the picture.

When Nadia and I first started working together, she was in the victim space. "I can't believe these people that I fight for are attacking me," she told me. She had to learn to question her impact and role in the various situations playing out in her department, so our first four months together, we focused a lot on accountability.

We had some difficult conversations in this space. She would tell me her team wasn't performing, and when I asked her what her part in the underperformance was, she would say, "I don't have a part."

"This is your team," I told her on the phone once. "If they're not performing, it's your problem." She hung up on me for that.

Despite some initial hiccups, she started to shift her mindset. One day, without prompting, she told me, "The lack of revenue this month is my fault. Though I'm still working on believing it, I can at least say it to you now."

Hallelujah! "So now what?" I asked her. "What do we need to get out of the way?"

Based on employee surveys we had done, we knew that her perfectionism was an issue for her team. Sometimes, the perfectionism was needed; a misplaced decimal, for instance, could have huge ramifications. However, Nadia's perfectionism extended to *everything*. Her team would develop a project plan that was 90 percent of the way there, and Nadia would handhold and micromanage them until they got to 100 percent. The result was a stifling of creativity and co-creation. There was no room for dissent with Nadia's leadership style: her way was the right way.

"Perfect" had become a label others applied to her. She was tall, beautiful, and physically fit, and she had a lot of energy that made her a pleasure to be around. Though it may seem nice to be called "perfect," positive and negative labels can be equally damaging. The harm occurs whenever we force ourselves into molds that do not reflect our truth. For Nadia, this idea of perfection seeped into many aspects of her life— her leadership, her appearance, her parenting. She struggled to live up to her own as well as others' ideas of perfection. The "perfect" label was imprisoning her.

Through our coaching, she used grace to look inside of herself and identify her gaps. After decades of compart- mentalizing, she began to integrate her soul into her work life. She became aware of the stories from her childhood that had become ingrained as fact. She'd grown up in poverty with a hypercritical father. He wasn't around a lot, and when he was, he liked things a very specific way. Nadia had learned to make things perfect so that her father would see her. If things weren't perfect, he either ignored her or yelled at her. Perfection equaled receiving love. If she wasn't perfect, she was unlovable and unworthy. Now, though she was making six figures and was objectively successful, she struggled with the same poverty mindset and drive for perfectionism from her childhood.

She started to shed those old behaviors, understanding that what served her as a seven-year-old no longer served her at forty. When you're seven, your ability to extrapolate the meaning of different experiences is limited, because you're only seven. Even seemingly good experiences can be written into your brain in harmful ways. As you become aware of and shift your patterns of behavior, old childhood traumas diminish and are rewritten with new neural pathways.

As Nadia delved into her childhood, she realized that she was doing to her daughter what her father had done to her. She broke down, horrified that her daughter might feel she had to be perfect to be worthy and lovable. This is what we do until we know better: we play out the same patterns that were imprinted on us as children. Once we know better, though, we can find another way. Nadia has been working on doing that with her daughter, repairing and redirecting their relationship. As a result, her daughter revealed that she didn't want to be in the school band and had only been doing it to make her mother happy. With Nadia's blessing, she decided to quit.

Nadia's professional life improved in similar ways. She

grew brave enough to examine how she came across to others with different ages, backgrounds, and status in the organization. She realized that she sometimes exuded an intimidating intensity and often used body language that was unconsciously demeaning.

Nadia started making changes. She began by extending grace to herself and then others. Her personal evolution soon had a wide impact.

NADIA'S EVOLUTION AND THE RESULTING CULTURE CHANGE

From the outside, it might have appeared as if Nadia were changing everything about herself. Really, she hadn't changed at all. She was who she always had been; she was simply allowing a more holistic version of herself to show up at work. Her team had always liked her for her intelligence and effectiveness as a leader; now they loved her for the person she was, because she was finally allowing them the opportunity to know that person. As they witnessed her humor and vulnerability, they began to respond with the same.

Nadia supervised over 170 people in a systemwide support function, and they were all affected by her transformation. These effects were not wishy-washy; they were concrete, objective improvements, measurable through two different employee surveys—a Leadership Culture Survey and an employee opinion survey—administered over three years.

In the Leadership Culture Survey that we executed in the first six months of our work together, 56 percent of Nadia's staff completed the survey, and 57 percent rated Nadia highly in controlling.

A year and a half later, we redid the survey. This time, 81 percent of the staff participated—a 44 percent increase. This much-higher employee engagement indicated that trust was building. Additionally, Nadia's controlling score reduced and showed her behaviors trending in a positive direction toward becoming a more creative leader.

In the company-wide annual employee opinion survey, Nadia had created a decrease of 70 percent of the concerns that had shown up the year prior. According to this survey, employees were now more willing to refer a friend to the team, felt stronger in their ability to receive the help they needed to complete their job tasks, and were better empowered to complete their work fully and accurately.

Nadia's personal transformation resulted in clear culture change within her organization. In addition to improved employee satisfaction, her department achieved impressive business results that culminated in a $65 million increase in revenue. They also exceeded the year goal at 102 percent, when the year prior, they had not met the target.

The change in Nadia was remarkable. Witnessing and supporting her through this transformation was one of the most humbling experiences of my coaching career. It was a metamorphosis that reminded me how resilient the human spirit is, and it proved how powerful grace is when we first extend it to ourselves and how transformative the resulting impact to a company's culture can be.

THE GRACEFUL TENETS IN ACTION: NADIA

About a year ago, Nadia called me up to say, "You know what I wrote in my gratitude journal today? I wrote that I'm grateful to whoever reported me to HR." Nadia was truly appreciative for the accusation, because it sparked her journey toward graceful leadership. The accusation revealed to her that the way people saw her was not the way she wanted to be seen and, most importantly, was not who she was in her internal landscape.

With this realization, she opened up to the coaching process and was courageous in looking at and seeking to understand her "less-than-desirable" parts. Through her exploration, she began to mature and develop in three graceful tenets in particular: evolving, transparency, and co-creating. (Remember:

We each work on different tenets at different times, and rarely do we ever work on all six at once.)

EVOLVING

Nadia was actually a very spiritual woman, and she wanted to better align her self and soul. However, she did not feel she could bring her soul to the office. How could she show tenderness and still hold a high level of accountability to the performance measures? If she showed caring for the person behind the job, would they see her as weak and take advantage? Would she compromise her authority?

These concerns are shared by many leaders for varied reasons. As emphasized in the compassionately powerful tenet, remember that compassion and power are not mutually exclusive. Like with all things, the key to evolving is boundaries and balance. Boundaries that are clear and consistent are vital to leadership at large and a key part of developing your grace as a leader.

Nadia and I began to explore how she could find more balance. We discussed how she could show more vulnerability with her direct reports to establish an appropriate level of intimacy—an intimacy that did not cross her or others' boundaries. She determined she could share personal stories and be more open about times she had failed, which was especially important considering people's impression of her as perfect. In this way, she showed her team that perfection wasn't real, even though she had created this illusion that it could and should be the goal. As she started to release her hold on how things "should" be, her grip on perfection loosened. With the burden of perfection lifted, her team began to bring problems to her attention before they became insurmountable, because they trusted that it was safe to do that.

Embracing this vulnerability and really embracing the evolving tenet was challenging and unnerving for Nadia. She was the only woman in her whole division at her level. Her whole career, she'd had only male role models. From them, she'd learned a command-and-control style of leadership that honored the organizational hierarchy—a leadership style that was no longer effective in an evolving multigenerational, multicultural workplace.

With exploration, though, she realized that the compartmentalization and misalignment of her work self and her soul was causing her deep pain. Specifically, some of her harmful patterns from childhood were being reinforced in her working relationships with her bosses. Just like with her father, she strove for perfection to please those with authority over her. She wasn't aware she was doing this until she realized that she was angry and didn't know why. She'd been with the company for twenty-four years at this point, so for twenty-four years she had been doing a version of the same thing she'd done at seven with her dad and with her boss at forty. This light bulb of understanding that she was causing herself pain by playing out old patterns gave her the motivation she needed to commit to grace.

It is important to note that while in this case she tied some of her behavior with her current bosses to outdated responses cultivated in childhood with her father, these are not "daddy issues." So often in our society we dismiss the simple fact that we all have opportunities to upgrade our operating system. Upgrading our operating system is not about fixing an emotional or psychological inability or defect; it is simply awakening to the areas in which we are ready to grow. It is hurtful to ourselves and others when we dismiss the area of our growth as undesirable or defective. This is one of the places grace has the opportunity to make the biggest impact. Acknowledging and embracing this process is a simple, kind, and graceful first act.

TRANSPARENCY

For Nadia, her biggest challenge in transparency was creating a distinction between others' labels and perception of her and who she truly was. She'd been told she was pretty and smart for essentially her entire life, so her identity was wrapped around those labels. People clearly liked those things about her, so her strategy was to be more of those things. This fractured her identity, because she was only being an edited version of herself: smart, pretty Nadia.

I asked Nadia to do a "word tattoo" exercise. She started with the silhouette of a body, and she wrote down all the words that people used to describe her. She quickly became uncomfortable and said, "I don't like these words."

"So what do you want to do about it?"

"I can't do anything about it," she said.

"Really?" I asked. We'd already gone through the victim chapter at this point, and I wanted her to remember and access her power.

"I don't know *how* to do something about it," Nadia clarified.

I decided to give Nadia a firsthand experience of how we can alter people's perceptions based on how we present ourselves. In our next group session, I came dressed in funky pants, mismatched socks, and platform Crocs. Nadia was horrified. She was like Jackie Onassis. She was always immaculately put together, with matching jewelry and freshly painted nails. She never left the house without makeup or had a hair out of place. She almost always wore heels, adding to her already commanding height. So she couldn't take her eyes off me as I walked in. I sat down and said, "We're going to talk about judgment today. Nadia gets to go first, because I want to know everything she thinks about my outfit."

She looked at me like a deer caught in headlights and owned up to the judgments that had passed through her mind. Later in the session, people talked about the kinds of judgments that people placed on her because of the way she dressed and presented herself. It was eye-opening for her. Some of the judgments people made about her were "good" (meaning that Nadia liked the perception), like people thinking that she was professional and well put together. Other judgments were not so good: "How much hairspray does she need? Are her eyelashes even real? Didn't pantyhose go out of style in the 1970s?" People thought she was stuffy and too concerned with her appearance.

Part of grace is being true to yourself and not conforming just to fit others' expectations. For most of my career, I felt pressured to dress a certain way, and only recently have I begun to dress in a way that is truer to myself. At the same time, the pinnacle of being graceful is understanding that different situations call for different aspects of who you are. If you're in front of the board of directors, you'll likely want to present a polished version of yourself, in a crisp suit. If you then need to sit down with one of your staff members whose child just passed away, you'll probably want to leave your suit jacket outside.

You can be authentic in the way you present yourself while also being aware of how the way you present yourself affects others' perceptions. Nadia liked dressing up, and she also wanted to be relatable. So she chose to make her wardrobe more casual in some situations. When she wanted people to be more relaxed, she swapped the heels out for flat shoes and wore a sweater instead of a tailored blazer. On her afternoon walks around the building, she put on sneakers. I remember one of her staff sharing that these walks were his favorite time to connect with her, as she was the most relaxed and even laughed a bit. She was still being true to herself, while doing it in a way that made people more comfortable. And she still broke out the heels and suits when they made sense for the situation.

> *The power to create the culture we*
> *want lies in authenticity.*
>
> —ROBERT J. ANDERSON AND WILLIAM
> A. ADAMS, *MASTERING LEADERSHIP*

As Nadia worked on transparency, she envisioned who she wanted to be, and she began building bridges between who she was showing up as and who she was inside. In no time at all, the bridges enabled the gaps to tighten, and her inner and outer selves became the same more than they were not. This transition is one that is both felt internally and witnessed externally. You do internal work and see your world shifting, and then those around you begin to see it too. This is where a leader starts to receive formal and informal feedback about the changes they have been experiencing internally.

Through her transparency Nadia became more relatable, and it changed her own life and also the lives of those around her. Nadia had a mentee, Dom, and their relationship grew much deeper as Nadia stepped into grace. Dom paid close attention to everything Nadia did. Not everything Nadia did fit well on Dom, though. Nadia was doing Nadia, and Dom was struggling to figure out what the Dom version of Nadia was. When Nadia relaxed her hold on perfection, Dom felt free to ask questions she had been afraid of asking previously, for fear of not being perfect and losing her spot as Nadia's mentee.

As a small example, one day Dom told Nadia, "You know, I don't really like sweater outfits."

Nadia's brow wrinkled in confusion. "Okay. Why are you telling me this?"

"Well, whenever we go to this type of meeting, you always wear a sweater outfit, so I've been doing it too."

"Oh! You don't have to do that."

As leaders, we forget that people are watching us all the time. If Nadia hadn't adjusted her leadership style, she never would have realized that Dom was buying sweater outfits she hated for meetings that she didn't need sweater outfits for. Instead, because of the safety Nadia had created, not only did Dom stop wearing sweater outfits, but she and Nadia also began to speak more openly about the ways Dom could become her own leader and not just mimic Nadia.

CO-CREATING

A big part of Nadia's journey was learning the power of stillness. She still has high executing functions and a propensity to jump into action, and she's also learned to discern when a situation calls for action and when it calls for stillness.

As soon as she started to sit back and give her team the space to think, feel, and do their jobs, interesting things began to happen. People took notice, and the CEO actually asked her to lead the innovation division for her area.

While Nadia had always been innovative by nature, her innovative nature had been hidden under her drive for perfection. As she released her grip on the hunt for perfection, which was always just out of grasp, she was able to allow herself to be in creative spaces more and more. She noticed that she would hum more and lose time in activities that required her inner innovator to show up.

As she experienced these moments of creative freedom, she also began to experience the grace she was offering herself and ultimately those around her. I remember a call where she shared that the grace she extended to self and others was like a big loop of love, and inside of it, accountability actually rose rather than diminished. Who would have thought that is how it works?

Because of Nadia's growth, her entire division started co-creating more. Her management team began working together more, and people were given access to projects and problems where before they had not been invited to the table. As a result, they were better able to get out in front of problems.

A GRACEFUL ENTRANCE BY A NEW LEADER

In chapter 5, "Use Grace to Distinguish Story from Fact," I mentioned Mara, who was fired from a hospital system because she couldn't let go of her command-and-control principles. After firing Mara, the hospital brought in a new leader, Drew, who was coming from a very successful hospital. Drew was a more graceful leader. She'd been doing a lot of leadership development, and she accepted this new job because she wanted a challenging environment to test her new skills and grow as a leader.

When she came in, she didn't try to change everything right away. Nor did she come in and clean house, which is the easy solution when you want to change a department's culture. The mark of a true leader is being able to transform a department or organization with the resources you have, not tearing everything down and starting from scratch.

Drew simply took the time to *be* with people. She gave them the space to get to know her, and she gave herself the space to get to know them. She identified the people who influenced without authority, and she started to win them over. She enlisted different people in co-creation so that they could show her the way instead of her dictating the way to them. She would say to people, "I don't know what I don't know. So you all show me what I don't know, and I'll show you what I do know that could help us be a better team."

Drew came in with compassionate power. She was definitely a heart-led leader. She was very approachable, and she also radiated a quiet power that made people respect her. Transparency was important to her. She was up front with people about why she'd been brought in and what she wanted to do. She set clear time frames. She outlined how long she would spend learning the department before they got into action, and then she indicated when she expected to see results based on that action. Because of this, everyone knew what to expect with her.

> *Leading for compassion can entail*
> *transformation and change all the elements*
> *of the organization's social architecture.*
> —MONICA C. WORLINE AND JANE E. DUTTON,
> *AWAKENING COMPASSION AT WORK*

Although it took some time, because her team had been

stuck in command-and-control leadership for so long, they eventually started to open up. Within a year and a half, it was a completely different department. The employee opinion scores rose, managers were working together to resolve challenges, and turnover was down. A promotion became an unintended consequence of the best kind. Her team supported her growth and trusted her handoff to a new leader, and she was able to stretch into the next level of leadership.

KEY TAKEAWAYS

Graceful leadership is not just an internal adjustment. It is also concrete actions that change how you and those around you show up for work. A single graceful leader can set off a domino effect of grace within an organization.

Grace encourages bravery in the wake of challenge and conflict. Graceful leaders confront their deficiencies head-on, resulting in both personal improvement and more effective leadership for their teams. Trust is a direct by-product of this behavior change.

Graceful leadership is about moving from an "I" to "we" mindset. Curiosity helps to achieve this, as curiosity allows you to express empathy and enables you to move along the infinity symbol to the location and way of being that each situation calls for. You will notice an ease to how you lead as grace settles into your being.

In the next chapter, we will examine how you can build your personal path into grace.

FURTHER READING

- *Awakening Compassion at Work,* by Monica Worline and Jane Dutton
- *Integral Life Practice,* by Ken Wilber, Terry Patten, Adam Leonard, and Marco Morelli
- *Mastering Leadership,* by Robert J. Anderson and William A. Adams

CHAPTER 8

CREATE YOUR UNIQUE PATH TO GRACEFUL LEADERSHIP

The first step to creating your path to graceful leadership is committing to the process. The catalyst that leads to grace can be internal or external. Maybe you've felt an inner calling that there has to be more, or maybe your boss or organization has told you that you need to make changes. Whether internal or external, once you are presented with the idea of grace and access to it within you, it is almost impossible to ignore. You may push it away for a year or two; however, grace will gently knock at your door until you open it. When you decide to respond to the calling of grace in your life and leadership, you will find that a synchronicity starts to come into your view to assist in your journey.

The initial commitment to grace can come from any direction. Eventually, though, to fully enter into grace, you must decide that *you* are worth the journey. At this point, your commitment will transform into a deeper why, which then evolves into your purpose. In Nadia's case, she started the work of grace because of external factors—an HR complaint and a directive from her superiors. As she did the work and realized the pain she was causing herself and others with outdated patterns of behavior, her why grew deeper. She wanted to become the best version of herself—the best leader, the best mother, the best Nadia—because she knew that *she* deserved it.

Whatever stage of the journey you're at, it's important to establish your why so that you can look for the best resources. Different whys will lead you down different paths of action. "Because my boss said to do it" will take you down one road; "I want to be ready for my next position" will take you down another; and "I want to be more fulfilled" will take you down yet another. If you want to become a more connected parent, you'll read different books than someone like Michael, who wanted to figure out how to integrate his spirituality into his work. Tailoring your resources to your why will allow you to make the most progress.

HOW I FOUND MY WHY

My why is to create safe spaces for souls to show up. It took me many years, with a lot of starts and stops, for me to uncover that why.

Like many, my first foray into self-development was thanks to an external catalyst. I was in my early thirties, working as a midlevel leader at a small consulting firm. One of the owners of the firm gave us all the option to go to a Landmark forum. Though I didn't really understand what was in it for me, I'm an avid learner and like to challenge myself, so I jumped at the opportunity. While it ended up not being for me, it did spark internal inquiry.

At this point, my why was simply to learn more about myself, because I was curious. This firm gave each of us a $1,000 stipend each year to learn whatever we wanted to learn and bring it back to the company. Because of this stipend, I discovered StrengthsFinder, which told me that I had a lot of influencing skills. This simple knowing helped me to understand so many things about why I was the way I was and set the foundation for me to accept and support my self while also creating a shift that aligned more with my inner landscape. With this, I was immersed into the integrating tenet and heading straight into the evolving tenet where I was determined to know, understand, and align to my mission and purpose in this lifetime. (Note: At the time, I had not yet created the tenets of graceful leadership and so was not aware that I was working on "integrating" and "evolving." I am applying this terminology in hindsight.)

The integrating and evolving tenets were hard work; however, they came pretty easily to me, without much internal or external resistance from myself, meaning that I did not experience much internal mental discomfort or difficulty adjusting my external behaviors. Even so, this work still took years and continues today. With so little resistance in these two tenets, I entered into the transparency tenet with excitement, and it all came to a screeching halt. This was (and, at times, still is) the tenet I struggle with the most. I have learned over the past decade in teaching these tenets that often one or two of the tenets will challenge people more than the others, with the most challenging tenets differing for each of us. For me, I had to and still have to feel worthy to be seen. The transparency tenet is all about aligning your walk and your talk. The great news is that most people who know me say this is now one of the things they value the most about me, as you do not have to second-guess where you stand with me. I have taken and become certified in several life-changing communication constructs along this path, and they have been invaluable in helping me with transparency. Transparency is all about seeing where you are not aligned and locating the resources you need to get unstuck. I do get stuck here once in a while, and I now have the tools and relationships I need—like my tribe of like-minded people—to know when I am stuck and then shift back into alignment. Remember: this is not about perfection; it is all about participation.

The tenet of connecting was one I worked on along with transparency. For me, they are very intertwined. This is not the case for everyone. We each have a unique path into our grace. This is the space that had me dive into gratitude and develop strategies and techniques for myself and others to access gratitude. Gratitude is the single best tool I have cultivated for the life I am living today. A gratitude practice opens up so many beautiful elements in life. It is the portal to understanding your purpose and how connected you are to everything else. Do not let the idea of its simplicity fool you. It takes a lot of grit to develop and recommit to your gratitude practice. Gratitude changes every single thing.

The co-creating tenet is one that was fun for me personally, as the work in the previous four tenets set this one up for me beautifully. It was no longer scary to collaborate and enlist others in problem-solving to develop new products and processes. Once you understand the "we" concept of connecting, co-creating makes more sense.

The sixth tenet—compassionately powerful—is one I love, as it removes the duality of being either compassionate or powerful. I remember wrestling with feeling compassion and knowing I had to show up powerful. It seemed as if showing up powerful removed the compassion. The journey into your grace will shine a light on this fallacy.

Throughout my work in all the tenets, I've been drawn to a

wide variety of resources. My how has included a little bit of everything. Because of my why, though, I've specifically been drawn to groups of people as a resource. If I want to create safe places for souls to show up, I need examples of how that is done. One of my core woundings is that I feel like I don't belong. It's something I still struggle with. So it's very important to me to find groups of like-minded people chasing the same thing together, so I have a place where I belong. When I can't find a group that addresses my needs, I create my own. In this way, my why and how intertwine in perfect synchrony, one supporting the other.

FINDING YOUR WHY

In *Find Your Why*, Simon Sinek says, "If we want to feel an undying passion for our work, if we want to feel we are contributing to something bigger than ourselves, we all need to know our WHY."

There's no prescribed way to find your why. Everyone has a different why, and everyone uncovers it in a different way. While true, that's not very helpful, is it? That's exactly why I created my second gratitude journal, which is about aligning who you are and what you do.

Just as my clients struggled to start a gratitude practice without structure, they had difficulty uncovering and communicating their purpose without guidance. The things you are grateful for are very telling, so gratitude can be a great path to your purpose. My second gratitude journal takes you right into your heart center. It's a perfect place to work out your why and is in fact designed to help you craft a personal mission statement.

You will know when you've found your why through your intuition. It will simply feel *right*. It will leverage more of your strengths than weaknesses, and it will inspire you. Additionally, when you start to share it with others, it will feel right to them as well. There will be a resonance, an echoing that comes back, reinforcing that your why is true to you.

FINDING YOUR HOW

Once you unearth your why, you will feel a craving to figure out your how—what path to take. Your how will be dependent upon your why. In my case, my job was to discover, "How can I create safe spaces? What does that look like to other people?" To do that, I did assessments. I hired coaches. I read a mountain of books. I participated in mastermind groups. I went to retreats. And I leaned on support groups of peers. With each new resource, I learned more and more.

> *The combination of your WHY and HOWs is*
> *as exclusively yours as your fingerprint.*
> —SIMON SINEK, *FIND YOUR WHY*

Just as we each have our own unique why, we each have our own how. Your how is an intimate thing that you will weave together for yourself. Assessments, coaches, books, mastermind groups, retreats, and support groups offer different benefits. Personally, I found a combination of all of them to be most effective. You may be drawn to some resources more than others. That's okay. You do not need to have the same how as me. Instead, leverage the available resources in the way that makes sense with your why. Also, hang out with other people uncovering their why and how. It is one of the most inspiring and supportive places to be.

ASSESSMENTS

Assessments are good when you want to create a common language—when you want to have an understanding of who you are in relationship to something else. I've never met the best assessment or the worst assessment. What makes one assessment stand out from another is your commitment to understanding it and digging out the gold from it.

Ultimately, assessments are a way to understand yourself. They can give you the words that help you describe yourself and even reveal things you didn't previously realize. Some of the assessments I've found helpful are StrengthsFinder, the Five Love Languages, 360-degree feedback, Myers-Briggs, Enneagram, Gene Keys, and even astrology and numerology. As an added benefit, many of these mentioned assessments have communities to help facilitate the learning and lead you to tribes of people on a similar path.

Whatever tool or data you use, the key is mastering its language and how the results manifest in you. For this reason, I recommend starting with just a couple of assessments at first. Diving deep into a single assessment can be more enlightening than dipping your toe into a dozen.

COACHES

Coaching is about guiding. A coach is someone who is able to ask the right question, at the right time, in the right way. An analogy I like to use is that coaches go around opening all the shutters and windows in your home in order to let light in. Then they invite you to come into your own house, through the front door. At that point, they ask, "Where do you want to go?" Maybe you say, "Well, I'm kind of hungry." So they say, "Let's go to the kitchen and make something to eat." Or maybe you're feeling tired, so they suggest you take a nap. Ultimately, it's your house, and you're setting the tone for the experience. The coach is simply guiding you.

Coaches have a multitude of tools you don't have, simply because this is what they do for a living. They help to lead you to the resources and experiences you need to progress. While a coach will guide you, you are the one who must ultimately do the work and follow through.

Many coaches will leverage assessments to help you find a new way to experience yourself and to create that common language mentioned earlier. Some assessments are fairly self-explanatory. As you get into the more-dynamic tools, you may desire and need someone to translate and offer context to the intention and flow of the assessment. It is very easy to make incorrect conclusions and assumptions when learning new tools.

To get the most from coaching, you must want to change *something*. The something could be any number of different things. However, if you don't truly want or aren't ready for a transformation, I suggest you start with reading books on the topic you are exploring and talking to others who have some expertise in the area you are seeking knowledge in. When you feel the burn to create real change and shift in your way of being, a coach is an invaluable tool.

Be thoughtful in choosing your coach. Find someone with whom you can connect and work well. Interview potential coaches before choosing one. When interviewing coaches, ask them what they're getting coached in themselves and what they're working on. That's a very revealing question. The best coaches have their own coaches (I always have at least one coach, and right now I actually have three), and they are always learning something new.

Once you make the commitment to a coach, stick with

them. As you delve into the work of coaching, you may experience moments of resistance. This is natural, and it can be tempting to avoid uncomfortable emotions by switching coaches. Reaching your full potential requires working through the uncomfortable, not running away from it.

THE DIFFERENCE BETWEEN COACH, CONSULTANT, AND THERAPIST

Coaches ask tough questions with great care, love, and respect. They *guide* clients; they do not prescribe solutions. They help people reach the next level, whether that is in terms of leadership or personal development. Coaching is focused on the future. Although coaching will use the past as a predictor for future behavior, it doesn't try to go back and heal or rewrite past traumas.

Consultants are brought in to solve a problem, not to help an individual grow, although that may be required as part of the solution. Consultants use their expertise to analyze situations and prescribe solutions. Coaches sometimes dip into consultation if needed, like when I helped José do a SWOT analysis. It is important to be clear what role you are playing with those you serve and to only play the role you are qualified for.

Therapists and coaches are similar in several ways. However, there are certain areas that only therapists are equipped to handle. Coaching does not involve a mental-health diagnosis. If you need help healing past trauma or handling a mental illness, you need a therapist, not a coach. To benefit the most from coaching, you need to start from a stable baseline of mental wellness. Sometimes you will uncover issues in coaching that you need to dig into with a therapist.

BOOKS

I have an extensive library. I have books on self-help, spir-ituality, performance, Six Sigma, process improvement, astrology, how to manifest your dreams, and so much more. I *love* books. They are the gateway to new worlds, new ways of thinking, and they allow us to challenge our belief systems in a safe and comfortable way. Books open up new possibili-ties, and who can't use more possibility in their life?

One of my fundamental beliefs is that if you're not learn-ing, you're dying. For me, I feel that if I'm not learning something new, I might as well just quit. Books are perfect for introducing yourself to new concepts. Books are rela-tively low risk and low effort. You can read a book about a new topic with no pressure or commitment. Even if I don't believe in UFOs, I can still pick up a book about UFOs and read it. When I'm done, I still might not believe in UFOs, and that's okay. However, I'll bet you I'll have learned *some-thing* that I can apply elsewhere in my life, like the power of questioning with curiosity.

A great thing about books is that they can be read at your own pace. You can take however much time you need to sit with a concept or reflect on different ideas. When I read, I like to take notes while I'm reading, and then after I finish the book, I set it aside for three days to a week. I then come back to my notes, take out what I want to integrate into my life, and leave the rest.

There's never a reason not to read. If you don't like the act of reading itself, try listening to audiobooks or podcasts instead. Read the books that resonate with you, and also be sure to read books that will challenge you and your way of thinking.

SUPPORT COMMUNITIES: PEER GROUPS AND MASTERMIND GROUPS

As you learn about yourself with assessments, coaches, and books, you come up with a theory—a hypothesis about yourself and how you want to move yourself into the future. A lot of theories and ideas will sound great in your head, and then, when you speak life into them or try to put them into action or some kind of framework, they dissolve. Theories need to be tested. Support communities are a great place to do that. They give you a safe place to practice your theories, acting as a litmus test.

A support community can be either a peer group or a mastermind group. The primary difference between the two is the intensity. A mastermind group is a formal group composed of individuals who come together to try to achieve certain results. The members of a mastermind group have similar, specific goals, and they meet regularly. For instance, I belong to a mastermind group of female entrepreneurs. We meet online every two weeks and gather face-to-face three times a year at a retreat to help one another toward our shared objectives of creating more revenue and becoming more community conscious.

In contrast, a peer group is less formal. They may meet with less regularity, and they may not have specific objectives, or different members may have different goals. A book club is typically an example of a peer group. It provides a space to challenge yourself and your beliefs by reading new books and discussing them with others. They offer the opportunity to test what you downloaded from a particular book and find out how your experience is unique or similar to someone else's. Book clubs can be really powerful if you have the right people and choose mind-expanding books.

Another important distinction is that mastermind groups are often pay-to-play, because usually there is somebody who facilitates the group. For this reason, along with the greater time commitment that mastermind groups require, I personally prefer to be part of only one mastermind group at a time. Over the years, I have been a member of four different mastermind groups. I entered into each one for a specific reason, and when that need was met, I moved on to another. Some common areas of focus for leaders are finances, entrepreneurship, branding/marketing, general business, networking, communication, and professional development. Find the group that will stretch you in the area you are looking to grow in.

Support communities are critical to stepping into grace.

Remember the six tenets; each of them has a community component. They give you a place to test and expand your ideas and consider new ways of thinking you previously hadn't. They also give you a place to belong, where you can share your struggles and receive encouragement. For many, this process is much easier when surrounded and supported by other like-minded people.

RETREATS

Retreats are an immersive experience—an incubator of rapid learning. A retreat could be a day, days, a week, or a month. The amount of time does not matter. There are also any number of retreats that focus on a variety of teachings. The defining feature is simply that you are there for a specific experience.

Because retreats are immersive, intensive, and experiential, they have the potential to be extremely transformative. The caveat is that you are able to take what you learn in the retreat and continue to apply it to your life following the retreat. Sometimes a retreat will be amazingly transformational in the moment, and then, when we return to our real life, we can't figure out how to make that experience stick.

You can go to a retreat at any point in your journey. Some people will attend a retreat after first delving into the subject matter through the other resources mentioned here.

Others will attend a retreat without any prior experience, wanting to immerse themselves into an entirely brand-new idea. This latter is what I did when I attended a seven-day silent retreat.

Twice a year, I have a "yes" month, where I say yes to everything that comes my way as long as it supports my mission statement and I have the resources to do it. During such a month, one of my coaches recommended I check out Adyashanti and dive in with a seven-day retreat. She knew it was one of my "yes" months, so I like to joke that she was cheating. Within two seconds of researching Adyashanti, I knew he was going to support my mission, and I had the funds. So I said yes.

I booked the retreat half a year in advance. When the time finally rolled around, I didn't want to go. I'd already paid, though, and once I pay for something, you can bet I'm going to attend. When I arrived at the retreat center, I met my roommate. The first night we were there, we were allowed to talk, and the first thing she asked me was, "How many spiritual retreats have you been on?"

I looked at her like she had four heads. "I'm not on a spiritual retreat," I said.

"Do you know where you are?" she asked.

Clearly I had no idea what I was in for, because I didn't even think about it as a spiritual retreat. Little did I know that it would change my whole life forever. I could write a book on that retreat alone. For now, it is enough to say that even as someone diving in with no prior knowledge and no idea what to expect, it was an incredibly rewarding experience.

If a retreat interests you, don't be held back out of fear that you don't know enough or won't fit in with the other participants. Beginner and expert alike can benefit from the same retreat.

THE IMPORTANCE OF INTEGRATION

All these resources—assessments, coaches, books, support communities, and retreats—are undoubtedly useful. However, it is the discipline and practice of integrating that education into one's leadership that actually engenders change. Simply put, you become a better leader through leading. I know that sounds obvious, yet so often leaders think that they can learn to be a leader in a bubble. They attend a training, go on a retreat, or earn a certification, and they think they will instantly be a new, better leader.

For every lesson you learn, you have to figure out how to make it work for you in a practical, real way or whether it will work for you at all. Some things will; some things won't. You must find those psychologies and methodologies that speak to you and then personalize them so that you can attain a living, breathing expression of the teaching. With every new thing I explore, I start by doing a lot of learning. Then I test the idea, practice it, refine it, throw away what didn't work, and incorporate what did. Only at that point do I move on to a new concept.

Give yourself time before jumping into the next thing. All your education won't matter if you leave everything you learn on the shelf. Be clear about what you want to learn and why you want to learn it. Then be intentional about integrating it into your life.

HONORING YOUR INTUITIVE NATURE

As you build your personal path to grace, awaken to your internal systems and body clues. Do not speed past these messages, which is what most of us do. I did this my whole life until the past decade or so. Have you ever walked into a situation where the hair on the back of your neck stood up? Maybe you ignored that feeling, brushing it off as a draft in the room. Then something or someone entered the room, and you were suddenly in a situation that was uncomfortable or, worse, dangerous.

On the other side of this, we also ignore good feelings. Think of a time you finally met a goal, small or big, after working really hard to get there. You likely feel elated inside, your chest expanding with joy. How long did you allow yourself to experience that feeling? Too many people don't even give it a nanosecond.

The things your body tells you are important. People call this internal body language by different names, like intuition or gut. Whatever you call it, take the time to listen, because this is where you will find your internal knowing. Your knowing is not about facts or data; it's about the things you know to be true on a deep level, as related to your soul and your purpose. This kind of knowing does not live in the head. It typically lives in the heart.

Mastery in most disciplines, including leadership, requires strong rational capability balanced by strong access to intuitive knowing.
—ROBERT J. ANDERSON AND WILLIAM A. ADAMS, *MASTERING LEADERSHIP*

I have made a conscious effort to allow my intuitive nature to have more influence over my life. Throughout my life, I would have an internal knowing and attempt to act on it. Then someone would ask me, "Well, how do you know it?"

"I just know it," I would reply.

They would shake their head at me and say, "If there's no data, you can't know it."

So I would dismiss my knowing. Inevitably, 99 percent of the time, after spending who knows how much time and money to do the research, the data would support my internal knowing. I had to learn to trust my intuition. This required a good deal of bravery. If I was going to insist that we not spend the time, money, and resources to get the data to support my internal knowing, then I had to own whatever consequences came of that.

People sometimes tell me that I take a lot of risks, like with my recent decision to transform my consulting business and move across the country. Sometimes you need to take risks to experience the most fulfillment from your life. I've also known for a long time that I don't need a big business. Even though I don't need or want a big business, I spent four years growing my consulting firm, year over year, over year, over year. That's what I thought I was supposed to do, because that's what "success" looks like, right? I kept pushing my intuitive knowing away. The more I focused on building my business, the more insistent my internal voice became. "You're putting your ladder against the wrong wall," that voice said. "Can you do this? Yes. It's not what you're here to do, though." I had to align my little self with my big Self in order to break that deeply ingrained belief system that growth and financial success were the goals.

Though it wasn't easy, I am now letting myself create some-thing more meaningful and sustainable for me. While it may look like a risk from the outside, it doesn't feel like one for me, at least not for my soul. That doesn't mean it's not scary. I left a million-dollar business in order to build a retreat center in the mountains of Vermont. There are a lot of uncertainties, and the fear can be paralyzing at times. When I sit in my body and my spirit—my intuitive knowing—I know it's the right thing to do, and I have no panic. Then I look at my bank account, and I slip into my head. Then the panic sets in. I have to deal with those moments as they arise and tune back into my intuitive knowing.

DIFFERENT PATHS TO GRACE

To help you see how different our paths into grace can be, I'll share two examples with you: Joe and Suzy.

JOE'S PATH TO GRACE

Joe was a senior director who thought he was ready to be VP. So his initial why that led him down the path of grace was a desire for career advancement. In order to make that happen, he did a 360 review to identify and work on his gaps. When he got his results, he was shocked. The review basically said, "You're a cold-hearted jerk."

Like a lot of people, Joe didn't know how to integrate his emotional capacity into his work world. If you went out fishing with Joe, you would know him as a sensitive being.

He rarely packed the fish home, instead preferring to release them so that they could get even bigger. He enjoyed teaching young people how to fish and was a kind, gentle teacher. If you later met him at work, you'd think it was his evil twin and not him. At work, he was walled off, with no access to the compassion he inhabited while fishing.

Initially, Joe resisted the results of his 360. He was confused and distraught. "I'm not a jerk," he told me, and he gave me countless examples—all involving his grandchildren, his fishing buddies, or a charity he worked with. It was true that he wasn't a jerk. At work, though, his compassion wasn't showing up.

During this time, Joe also had the support of a savvy, emotionally intelligent leader. This leader was moving in the direction of grace themselves, and they cleared the way for Joe. This leader made it clear that if Joe wanted to advance, this emotional work was a requirement, and the leader did it in a way that enlisted Joe to do the work both for the organization and for himself.

As a result, Joe agreed to work with me as a coach. He completed an emotional intelligence assessment so that we could have a common language to work through the integration he would be exploring for the work we would do. He scored low on self-awareness, and that made him dig in. It's easy to dismiss others' feedback, like with his 360.

This was a self-assessment, though. This wasn't someone else telling him he had low self-awareness. He was telling *himself* this. He accepted the issue and wanted to understand what it meant and how to "fix it." His why deepened from wanting to advance in his organization to wanting to heal his internal gaps.

For Joe, it was great to start with assessments and coaching because he needed the structure and guidance. Since he resisted others' feedback, it was also important that his how include *self*-assessments, since it is harder to resist one's own feedback. To further tailor his how, we used a lot of military books that showed compassion could work. He was former military himself, and his military background played a big role in his leadership. Seeing grace and compassion in the frame of the military gave it credibility for him.

A big part of Joe's why was still career advancement, so he incorporated small experiments as part of his how. His biggest gap was a failed integration between his personal self and work self, so he ran these experiments simultaneously at work and at home. He found out, interestingly enough, that the experiments succeeded at work as well as they did in his personal life. He'd simply never thought to try these things at work before. As an example, one experiment was celebrating achievements. When his grandson was in a play and did a great job, it was natural for Joe to celebrate with him. So he did the same thing at work when an employee did a good job, and guess what? The employee liked it and appreciated it just as much as his grandson did. (Note: How they celebrated was certainly different; nonetheless, it was a celebration.)

With these experiments, he was able to see clear improvements in his work and in himself. The artificial walls he'd built between his personas began to fall down, and his emotional quotient rose. A lot of people at his work didn't think it was possible for Joe to become a more graceful leader. That was only because they'd never seen Joe outside of work. Joe already had all the skills he needed; he just needed to integrate them into his work. This is true for everyone. We already have everything we need. It's just a question of whether we're willing to allow those things to show up. Often this requires the hard work of facing fears that are a lifetime old and the limiting beliefs that support them—not for the faint of heart!

I coached Joe for almost nine months, and then he ran with his skills for another three months on his own. At the twelve-month mark, he redid his 360 review. He'd cut his gaps in half. That's huge movement for a year. He also redid his emotional intelligence test, and his self-awareness score went up. With all of this, he was experiencing more fun and joy in his work life. He shared that he was excited to express appreciation for others and looked for opportunities all the time now. He even took a few folks on his team out deep-sea fishing. The cherry on top? He got the promotion!

SUZY'S PATH TO GRACE

Suzy had recently been promoted from supervisor to manager. In her previous role, she'd primarily been an informal influencer. As soon as she was given the formal authority, she went rogue. She went from being a peer who was collaborative to a command-and-control leader who made demands and wore the micromanaging badge with pride.

Before she'd been in the role for a year, she started to get HR complaints, and I was brought in for coaching. With Joe, the coaching was a proactive strategy to prepare him for his role; with Suzy, it was a reactive response because she hadn't been set up for success before her promotion. Unsurprisingly, she scored very low on her initial emotional intelligence assessment, especially in empathy. That was to be expected, because she didn't have any prior training or a good role model like Joe did.

Initially, she was hungry for her boss's approval, so she actually welcomed my help as a coach. She'd seen the results of my working with others in the company, so she had a high level of trust in me. While she was angry that she'd been set up to fail, she mostly felt lost. She didn't know what to do. She knew she had to do *something* different, though. That formed her initial why for starting this process.

Besides assessments and coaching, Suzy's greatest resource was a peer support group. When informal influencers are promoted into formal authority, they often shift from a collaborative to competitive mindset, eroding their peer groups. I asked Suzy to create two relationships for her peer group—one with a person she wanted to have a relationship with and one with a person she wouldn't typically want to create a relationship with. These two individuals were pivotal to her success. They gave her support and helped her find a balance in her leadership.

With all these resources, Suzy was able to turn things around and start performing at the level she and her bosses wanted. She began creating healthy work relationships at all levels. The performance of her team continued to rise as she became more proficient and delegated, holding accountably through relationship, not just metrics. Her self-confidence grew as she was asked to partner in new and innovative ways with her peers and other teams. Steadily and surely, she opened to the graceful leader within her, resulting in positive impact for the business at large.

KEY TAKEAWAYS

When you begin building your own path to grace, resistance will likely come up. It's important to work through this resistance, because what we resist persists. If you can be still and curious, the resistance will subside. You can then continue forward on your journey.

There are so many resources available to you. To get the most out of them, do things deeply. Don't jump from coach to coach or from book to book looking for a silver bullet. The silver bullet doesn't exist. What will take you to the next level is delving deep.

You are constantly evolving, and so your path to graceful leadership must constantly evolve with you. Graceful leadership is a never-ending, always refining process. Just when you get to the perceived end, you see a bend in the road to take another tour. The difference is you are not the you that took the tour last time, so it is over and over again anew.

As you step into graceful leadership, you will become a beacon for others, with the power to transform entire organizations. In the next chapter, we will look at when and how to discuss grace in your workplace.

FURTHER READING

- *Find Your Why*, by Simon Sinek
- *Gratitude Journal*, by Alexsys Thompson (available at www.alexsysthompson.com/product-category/journals-books)
- *The Future of Management*, by Gary Hamel

CHAPTER 9

HOW TO TALK ABOUT GRACE IN YOUR WORKPLACE

A lot of work environments don't have a platform or language to access connectedness, love, compassion, and empathy. As a result, these heart-centered forums either do not exist in the organization, or if they do, they're not respected or understood. With this kind of resistance, it can be difficult to know how to talk about grace or whether it is appropriate to talk about it at all.

IS YOUR ORGANIZATION READY?

To discern how ready your workplace is to have a dialogue

about grace, start by taking inventory of how people hold conversations with each other. Is conflict something that explodes into fights, something that is avoided, or something that is addressed and moved through with mutual respect? If conflict escalates into fights, your workplace is probably not ready for a conversation about grace. If conflict is avoided, your organization may be closer to ready yet still not quite there. If people are willing to engage with conflict from a place of love, kindness, and respect, then your organization is already demonstrating some level of grace. This is a good sign that your organization is ready for a conversation about grace.

Another thing to look at is your organizational chart. Is the leadership structure all up and down, or is there a lattice? Can people move across departments, or do people only move up, not sideways? Is there cross-training? Do teams have communication between multiple layers of leaders, or do VPs only talk to VPs and senior directors only talk to senior directors and so on? An organization that has a strict up-and-down structure with little communication and interaction between departments and leadership levels is typically less graceful than one with a lattice structure and open movement and communication between different teams and levels. Remember our infinity symbol and how a graceful leader is called to move effortlessly to whatever position is needed—a latticed structure can offer the same idea to the organization at large.

You can also assess your organization's readiness using the six tenets of graceful leadership. If your organization has access to or demonstrates three or more of the graceful tenets on a regular basis, then it is likely ready for a conversation about grace. Grace won't show up where an organization isn't ready, so if you see grace, it means your organization is ready. You can also start conversations around the six tenets to test the willingness of your organization to explore the concepts.

Whatever your organization's level of readiness, be clear about where your organization is, and meet them where they are. A graceful leader doesn't push the agenda. If you decide you want to run a marathon, you don't just go out and do it. You have to train and work up to longer distances. If you've already been running for a while, maybe you can start with an eight-mile run. On the other hand, if you haven't run since high school PE, you might need to start with just a mile or even start by walking.

A key point to remember here is that grace can and does exist in pockets of organizations. It does not have to be an all-or-nothing experience. The readiness of an organization is a sliding scale. In some areas, your organization may be ready for discussions of grace, and in others, it may not be. For example, maybe it's a conversation you can have with a single leader even if you can't have it with your whole team. Or maybe you can talk about certain aspects of grace and not others. You will need to examine each individual situation to determine the suitability of discussing grace. For simplicity's sake, though, I'm going to discuss two categories of ready vs. not ready and what you can do in each case.

MY ORGANIZATION ISN'T READY—WHAT DO I DO?

It is not a good idea to force conversations about grace, as not all organizations are safe for this kind of conversation. That doesn't mean they won't eventually be ready, though. In fact, grace is a seed that one person can plant, and it can then begin sprouting in other areas of the organization. This is a personal journey, and your willingness and capability to be the pioneer is simply your call.

Graceful leadership is a way of being. If your organization isn't ready to talk about grace, the best thing you can do is simply be a graceful leader. If you start espousing things and pushing an agenda, you'll increase resistance. Instead, lead by example—a core competency of the graceful leader. In this way you can plant and nurture the seeds of grace, and eventually, your organization may become ready. As Gandhi said, "If we could change ourselves, the tendencies in the world would also change. As a man changes his own nature, so does the attitude of the world change towards him." More succinctly, "Be the change you want to see in the world."

A graceful leader does not have to declare that they are graceful. It is simply understood and experienced. When you are graceful, other people will begin to take notice. They will get comfortable with what grace looks and feels like. They may even begin to use you as a model. Over time, they may become ready to pursue grace themselves.

Even if you are just being graceful and not talking about grace, you may still face resistance. For instance, if you try to co-create, you may bump up against an organizational chart that strives to keep people in their roles. The graceful leader blurs the lines between different roles. A senior VP who is a graceful leader might decide to bring together an analyst from HR, a senior accountant, and a salesman to work on a problem together. Though these people are not all VPs, they have the specific skills, knowledge base, and experience that the graceful leader needs to co-create. The organization may push back against that, seeing it as inappropriate or not helpful.

> *Being still does not mean don't*
> *move. It means move in peace.*
> —E'YEN A. GARDNER

If you experience pushback, don't get caught up in the drama. Cultivate stillness so that you can respond and not react. You may have to adjust your tack slightly and find a way to co-create while also navigating your organizational chart.

In addition to being graceful, you can also talk *around* grace.

While talking directly about grace might trigger too much resistance, you could talk about ways to handle conflict or give feedback. You can essentially talk about graceful ways of being without ever once saying the word *grace*.

While being graceful *is* work, it's work that is so rewarding and exhilarating, not exhausting. Especially when you are a newly graceful leader, an organization that isn't ready for grace can be incredibly damaging. The toughest part for leaders who lead through grace is their inner desire to remain in an organization, relationship, or community that does not show any interest in also embracing grace. If you are evolving and stepping into grace and your organization or certain people in your organization are pulling you back into harmful habits, consider leaving. While a graceful leader can have a huge impact on an organization, an ungraceful organization can also have a damaging impact on a graceful leader. You may not be ready to take on an ungraceful organization, and that's okay. Sometimes you need to prioritize your personal journey so that you can better help others later.

MY ORGANIZATION *IS* READY—WHAT NEXT?

If your workplace is ready to talk about grace, that's great! Maybe there are already strong servant leaders or conscious leaders at your organization. Graceful leadership is then an easy next step. Once you begin the conversation of grace, patience and a commitment to it will be vital to your personal health and ability to stay the course.

When leaders set off on a path to graceful leadership, they often think that grace means religion. Religion is an especially difficult topic to navigate in the workplace, so they struggle with the idea of incorporating grace into their work, let alone talking about it. They fear that, if they were to talk about it, they would alienate others or be alienated themselves because of their religious faith. In fact, when I was working on the title for this book, I was told by many well-intentioned people to remove the word *grace* and find a word that was more "acceptable." I was still for a while with that and ultimately resilient, believing that we are ready for—and, more than that, *need*—graceful leaders to lead us into the new world that is evolving.

Remember: grace does *not* mean religion. For you, your religious faith may be a part of grace, even a big part. However, grace alone is simply the connection to soul, spirit, and heart. Talk of religion can make people uncomfortable, and that isn't graceful. So in any conversation about grace, an important first step is *defining* grace. Grace is the experience of a loving, connected compassion within yourself. This way you can ensure that you don't inadvertently alienate anyone.

Talking about grace can be as easy as saying, "Hey, let's talk about..." There are any number of entry points into a conversation about grace. You can introduce grace as a concept in itself, or you can choose a single tenet of graceful leadership to discuss. You could share this book if you want or encourage people to start a gratitude practice.

Once you break the ice, you can move into deeper conversations. Looking around at self and others, not from a judging perspective, you can begin to discuss with others how grace is showing up in your organization and what kinds of things you would like to focus on moving forward.

In my experience, grace calls itself in. You don't have to push it in. Once grace starts to show up in an organization, conversations about it will happen organically.

> *Grace is an energy; not a mere sentiment; not a mere thought of the Almighty; not even a word of the Almighty. It is as real an energy as the energy of electricity. It is a divine energy; it is the energy of the divine affection rolling in plenteousness toward the shores of human need.*
>
> —Benjamin Jowett

To further help you understand when your organization is ready for grace—and when you are ready to step into graceful leadership—I will share two examples from my own life, one where I found grace to be unsustainable in my current organization and another where I was able to fully step into my power as a graceful leader.

THE JOURNEY INTO GRACE: IT CAN BE BUMPY

Embracing graceful leadership was a process that required honesty about what I could and could not handle. One of my early forays into graceful leadership involved working with a peer VP, Heather.

A client wanted both Heather and me to work on their project. Heather worked on the IT side of the office, and she and I had spent most of our work relationship competing against each other. We didn't particularly like each other, and we typically didn't work together. However, the client was adamant.

At this time, I was receiving coaching. My coach looked at my StrengthsFinder report and then at Heather's. "This isn't going to work," she told me. Then she took me through the results and explained that Heather and I were like oil and water. I'd felt this intuitively, and now I had a concrete report to tell me why. It wasn't that Heather was bad or that I was. We were just wired very differently. Our strengths and deficiencies lined up perfectly to make us butt heads.

Working with Heather forced me to evolve. My grace was tested and put through the fire. Heather and I had to innovate and co-create, and we ended up formulating a great solution for the client that brought in a lot of money. Our working relationship ended up being positive for both the client and our company. And yet...it was *not* positive for me. In fact, it was *exhausting.*

I wasn't yet mature enough in the areas I needed to be to make the relationship work on a long-term basis. Yes, I'd managed to work with Heather on this project, and it had sucked the life out of me. It took too much time and energy, and I knew I couldn't keep it up forever. That was hard to accept. I'd been working so hard on being graceful, and now it felt like I was taking a giant step backward.

It was difficult to not feel like a failure. However, grace must be sustainable. If I forced myself to keep working with Heather, I would burn out. It would be like trying to swim against a rip current. Eventually, I'd exhaust myself completely, and I would be pulled back into limiting beliefs and behaviors; the work I'd done would slowly be dismantled. I had to extend grace to myself. As much as I hated to admit it, I wasn't ready. And the organization wasn't ready either. I would have had to force myself to be graceful and push grace on others. By definition, this isn't graceful. Instead of fighting against the rip current, I chose to swim parallel and break out of it. I left that organization, and it ended up being one of the best decisions I made.

INVITING GRACE IN: WHEN THE CHALLENGE IS JUST RIGHT

Not long after leaving the company where I worked with Heather, I was brought in to work with the HR team at my city's newspaper. The team was gun-shy, exhausted, and not terribly productive. My old self would have come in and immediately jumped into action, whipping them into shape using command and control. Instead, I asked a lot of questions and simply observed.

Before I was even hired, one of the things I'd noticed was that the HR office was downright depressing. It was a sterile, dank, unpleasant place. Nobody wanted to spend time in HR, and with that kind of office, I didn't blame them. As part of my negotiation before accepting the job, I requested money to redecorate the HR office. It was like a signing bonus, for the whole staff and not just myself. Though the recruiter looked at me like I might have a screw loose when I made the request, I got the redecorating fund.

We redid the entire office. We repaired and reupholstered some cool vintage pieces of furniture, and we hung some of the award-winning photography from the newspaper. The change was like night and day. The HR office became a destination, not just where people went when they were in trouble. It was like a Starbucks lounge instead of the principal's office. A good number of people would come down to HR to have their morning cup of coffee and chat. We found out more about what was going on in the organization through these morning chats than we'd ever been able to find out before.

It was exactly what the HR department needed, and it didn't require any dialogue with others about grace. I simply showed up as a graceful leader and invited grace in. Although there were still challenges—like when I later had to fire the entire staff of our sister newspaper, as detailed in chapter 3— they were not exhausting like they'd been at my previous job.

Even though I ultimately was let go from this job, I feel that I was able to make a lasting impact. In setting an example of graceful leadership, I was able to start ripples of grace in others' lives. So if your organization isn't ready for a conversation about grace, don't fret. You can have immeasurable impact simply by being a graceful leader.

KEY TAKEAWAYS

Knowing your audience is key when opening up conversations about any new ideas or concepts. Before you talk about grace, take an inventory of your organization to assess its readiness for such a conversation. It may be better to teach grace by example instead of by language.

A graceful leader is unifying and understands the power of language, always using it to build, not break relationships. In starting conversations about grace, be sure to define grace clearly. Otherwise, people may mistake it for religion and be uncomfortable with the idea. Grace is a unifying energy, not a divisive one. Throughout the dialogue, deploy the skill of curiosity. This will ensure that you're actually having a conversation and not simply lecturing at people.

For this chapter, I am not including any further reading. All the resources listed in the previous chapters will give you a strong foundation. Now is the time for you to take all that you've learned and begin to put it into action. You never stop being a student in graceful leadership, but as you begin to transform your organization, you step into the role of teacher as well as student. The future of the conversation about graceful leadership will be driven by you and other graceful leaders. So don't rely only on existing resources. Create your own!

PULLING IT ALL TOGETHER

Graceful leadership is a powerful, transformative way of being. When we are fully in our grace, we are unshakable. We know when to lead from any position that is needed and how to get there. Storms will come, and we will navigate through stillness until it is time for action. We will charge forward to create safety for our team or let them lead and hold back to offer support as needed. Grace is the most potent and powerful way of being. Grace is heart centered and aligned to you, your mission, and your belief system and allows all others to be in the same place without needing to make them wrong.

Each of the six tenets of graceful leadership offers real, tangible benefits. There is a tear-out page of these tenets at the back of the book, or head over to my website for a printable PDF to post and share: www.alexsysthompson.com/6-tenets.

By integrating your mind, body, and soul, you can break down the artificial walls you've built between the different versions of you. Partitioning yourself cuts you off from your full power. By removing these barriers, you will have access to all your myriad strengths.

Transparency is the key to clear communication, which is the foundation of any healthy relationship, whether it be a personal or work relationship. When you have transparency with self and others, you eliminate confusion. You know who you are, and so do the people around you.

Evolving your alignment of soul and self will bring you in alignment with your purpose. Purpose gives us meaning and fulfillment. If you want lasting happiness, purpose is the key.

When you are connected with yourself and others, you transcend from an "I" perspective to a "we" perspective. Whether you are aware of it or not, we are all connected. If you choose to remain trapped in an "I" perspective, you will still have an impact on the world around you; however, you will have little control over what that impact is. By tapping into this connection, you can ensure that your impact on the world is intentional, creative, and impactful.

Becoming a co-creator lets you find innovative solutions. As individuals, we are limited. Together, we can accomplish incredible feats. Think of any of humankind's greatest achievements—the eradication of deadly diseases, putting a man on the moon, the creation of the internet. A *team* of people will always be more powerful than a single individual, and co-creation is not limited to people alone. It is also available with nature.

In embracing compassionate power, you become a true leader, not an enforcer. Pushing and pulling people will only get you so far. Your ability to remove duality and hold compassion and power equally will lead to a team, outcomes, and a life you will love.

Graceful leadership has huge personal and professional benefits. If your organization is doing soul-filled work, the work gets easier and more fun, and the work environment feels peaceful instead of stressful. And believe it or not, grace will become a vital part of how you achieve those coveted results, whatever they may be.

THE URGENT NEED FOR GRACEFUL LEADERSHIP

In my experience, we have too much fear in the world today. We see it on social media, in the news, in our politics. In many ways, fear does the opposite of grace. It makes us retreat into ourselves and build walls. It kills compassion and curiosity. It distracts us from purpose.

The antidote to fear is grace. Anywhere you have a community where people are offering grace, you have love, and love replaces fear. In a time when fear is rampant, we could certainly use more love. Fear's power diminishes in the presence of grace. While the fear doesn't disappear completely, it becomes manageable. You are able to identify it and resolve it with the appropriate tenets of graceful leadership.

We *need* graceful leaders because graceful leadership triggers a domino effect of impact. Changing yourself allows you to change your organization. Changing your organization changes your community. Changing your community changes the world. As Bob Chapman said, "This is how we can start to heal our brokenness: sending people home as better spouses, parents, children, friends, and citizens of their communities."[7]

It's difficult to feel as if we have power as individuals. When you tap into grace, though, your power grows exponentially. You can do far more through grace than you can do with your personal strength alone. The untold truth of this transformation is that as you align more with your inner grace, your desire and need for power as you may have previously related to it diminishes greatly.

---

7   Monica C. Worline and Jane E. Dutton, *Awakening Compassion at Work* (Oakland, CA: Berrett-Koehler, 2017), 173.

CONTINUE ON YOUR PATH

This is the point in the book where I'm supposed to tell you to go out and start on your path to graceful leadership. You've already started, though, simply by picking up this book. Now you simply need to continue.

You have absolutely nothing to lose by continuing down the path of graceful leadership. You don't lose any part of yourself. You don't lose power. You don't lose results. They all live within the grace that is you.

You can only gain a fuller access to all you are by entering into grace. Remember that grace is a creative, not destructive, power. Grace gives you freedom. It unlocks all that you are, and it removes the noose from around your neck that is calling you into being something you don't want to be. With this freedom, you can make better choices, and your achievements will be beyond what you can imagine for yourself and your organization right now.

They say that the most important step in any journey is the first one. In reality, it's not the first step; it's the *next* step. Right now, all of *you* is waiting on the other side of grace. Your purpose is waiting. A more productive, collaborative team of employees is waiting. A better world is waiting. So what's it going to be? What's your next step?

GRATITUDES

Life is full of treasures. You simply need to look for them. Along this amazing life I am living, I have been privileged to meet and know some extraordinary humans who have demonstrated grace as a way of being. Following are a few of them for whom I would like to express my reverence. Knowingly or not, they came into my life at impressionable times and have had a great impact on my journey into my inner grace.

First and foremost, I extend my gratitude to you, the reader, and all the grace within you. Simply by picking up this book, you have started your journey into grace. I have no doubt that as you continue on that journey, you will achieve beautiful, remarkable things. Thank you for all your time and thoughtfulness as you have traveled through these pages.

Mark Benoit was one of my first memorable experiences with grace in human form. In my early twenties, I had the pleasure to work with Mark in the car business—he ran the finance division. Not sure about you, but that role doesn't conjure up warm fuzzies and trust for me. Mark, however, was different. He was a man of stature for sure; however, he was able to create a place for you just to be with him, his voice deep and slow and intentional. When he asked questions, he was genuinely interested in your answers. It wasn't just small talk to close a deal, and he was never in a hurry. He was someone who knew who he was and as a result let you be wherever you needed to be, never projecting his view on you. His movements, his tone, and the compassion you experienced through his beautiful blue eyes were all mesmerizing and made you feel safe. The grace he gave so freely to everyone was and continues to be a huge gift he offers this world. Thank you, Mark, for being a safe, loving, and grace-filled place for me for over thirty years.

Kay Taylor is a powerful and intense being. She has been a coach for me over the past five years, and she meets me where I am. I so craved a female leader in my life who could and would meet me with just as much (or more) power than I brought. Kay demonstrates compassionate power in her very existence. She has a life-giving ability to be with you and hold the possibility you see for yourself, with an unwavering belief in your ability to live into that possibility. I have asked Kay some questions that I would never ask another human, as I would not trust the answers they would offer. Where others would step on eggshells, for fear of sharing something they think I wouldn't want to hear, Kay gives me the gift of honesty. I value Kay for her ability to share what she sees and not become attached to it, viewing it as simply a data point in a moment in time. This mindset is a valuable tool I have been able to refine for myself in my work and in my internal grace-filled landscape. I am eternally grateful for her presence in my life and our world.

Curt Liesveld is now an angel among us, having shifted into our spirit realm. However, I still spend approximately an hour a week with him and more in the growing season. We both love to garden, and I treasure the insights and companionship he has shared with me. He has a special place at Ubuntu. He is a co-creator here, with an active part in the evolution of this sacred place. Curt came into my life and was able to see through a mask I had been wearing my whole life. It was shocking to be seen in this way. I can remember the moment in time that he saw me peek from behind the mask. He gently invited me into conversation from there, and I eventually came out from behind the mask to connect in his grace-centered space. From there we cultivated a gentle, compassionate friendship that felt familiar and so welcome. The gift of being seen is one of the greatest gifts there is. It is a pillar of who I have become and will continue refining into. With a full and blessed heart, I express great reverence for Curt.

ABOUT ALEXSYS

My life's mission is to create safe spaces for souls to show up. Throughout my life, it's manifested in a variety of ways: friend, mother, partner, leader, entrepreneur, executive coach, conflict resolutionist, keynote speaker, author, intuitive, integration coach, and evolving human.

People amaze me in all kinds of ways. I tend to see their aura (their truest nature) and all the possibility that exists there. As a result, my executive/integration coaching practice has evolved significantly to include the essence of the whole being. For every amazing soul I'm blessed to support, I weave together a unique combination of tools, with each coaching relationship starting with a gratitude practice. Time and time again, I see that this is the key that opens all the other doors within a person for exploration.

I love nature and animals; my current interest is in becoming a master herbalist. I love to read. I lose time writing and working in the garden. I enjoy creating physical spaces that nurture community, conversation, and connection. I treasure the early morning quiet time with a cup of warm tea, my gratitude practice, and meditation to set the pace for the day, and often wonder why it took me so long to make this my ritual.

I am a dreamer who dove off into the dream without a parachute, trusting my wings would unfold as I descended. Ubuntu—a safe haven—is the three-dimensional realization of this lifelong dream that I have been living into. Ubuntu is an intensive and intimate place in the mountains of Vermont to come and reconvene with your soul and work the tenets of graceful leadership. I bring my mission to create safe places for souls to show up into reality every day when I work with leaders and teams. I am excited to continue this purpose through Ubuntu, offering a place for souls to show up and do their work with me and their own inner guidance system through several programs that we are developing as I write this. We start with you leading you and work from there, helping you to reunite with your grace-filled center. It is one of the most transformative and life-affirming journeys you will embark on during your lifetime. For more information, head over to www.ubuntuasafehaven.com.

The 6 Tenets of Graceful Leadership

Alexsys THOMPSON

INTEGRATING: MIND, BODY, AND SOUL
- knows and can communicate their own mission and vision/purpose
- understands and is aware of internal body (health), as well as the messages their body language communicates, and manages both
- connects to a power larger than self, serving the collective goodness

EVOLVING: ALIGNMENT OF SOUL AND SELF
- is relentless in the pursuit of understanding and aligning self to purpose
- is a constant learner who is gentle in all pursuits, enlisting a lens of curiosity with a focus on integration
- creates relationships that have balance with giving and receiving and does both themselves

TRANSPARENCY: SELF AND OTHERS
- demonstrates authenticity in their behavior and communication (they walk their talk)
- is an active listener and is open, clear, and consistent with their message and its consequences
- doesn't base sense of self in labels or others' perceptions (they allow the people that follow them to see their heart, and they lead from this consciousness)

CONNECTING: SELF AND UNIVERSE
- has moved from the "I" construct of being to a "we" construct (the "we" is universal, not just humanity)
- has discovered and developed an inner guidance system that is connected to the collective
- demonstrates empathy and gratitude

CO-CREATING: INNOVATIVE
- seeks new ways of solving problems that are nontraditional to the way their profession/ organization does
- surrounds themselves with talent different from theirs and people competent in areas they are not
- demonstrates the ability to both lead and follow, all while maintaining the leadership role

COMPASSIONATELY POWERFUL: IN ALL THINGS
- influences through an open heart and clear agenda, blending stillness and action
- understands and owns the impact and consequences of their behavior to self/organization/ world
- creates room for flow while maintaining structure